FROM MORNING TO NIGHT

Domestic Service in
Maymont House
and the
Gilded Age South

FROM

Morning

TO

Night

Elizabeth L. O'Leary

Elizabeth L. O'Leary

UNIVERSITY OF VIRGINIA PRESS

CHARLOTTESVILLE AND LONDON

University of Virginia Press

© 2003 by Maymont Foundation

All rights reserved

Printed in the United States of America on acid-free paper

First published 2003

9 8 7 6 5 4 3 2 1

LIBRARY OF CONGRESS CATALOGING-IN-PUBLICATION DATA

O'Leary, Elizabeth L.

   From morning to night : domestic service in Maymont House and the gilded age
South / Elizabeth L. O'Leary.

     p.   cm.

Includes bibliographical references and index.

ISBN 0-8139-2160-0

   1. African American women domestics—Virginia—Richmond.   2. Women
domestics—Virginia—Richmond.   3. Dooley family.   4. Maymont (Richmond, Va. :
Dwelling)   I. Title.

HD6072.2.U52 V865 2003

975.5'451'0410922—dc21   2002013488

FRONTISPIECE: *A Reflective Pause*, Doris Walker Woodson, 2002 (Private collection;
photo by Katherine Wetzel)

To the men and women who kept Maymont House, 1893–1925,
and to their descendants and friends who kept their stories alive

The housekeeping in every department should move like perfect, well-oiled machinery, with invisible wheels. . . . Let the comforts and luxuries provided for your family and guests come to them as by magic; let them hear no preparatory sounds, and see no sights that shall take from the freshness of the entertainment.

ELIZABETH MILLER, *In the Kitchen* (New York, 1883)

I am invisible, understand, simply because people refuse to see me. . . . When they approach me they see only my surroundings, themselves, or figments of their imagination—indeed, everything and anything but me.

RALPH ELLISON, *Invisible Man* (New York, 1952)

My grandfather went to work to do a job, but to do it invisibly. To have control of situations, get the job done, "come and serve me, but be quiet about it." But at home he was our "Papa." He was not invisible to us. He was the heart of our family, our moral compass.

MARY TWIGGS, granddaughter of Maymont head butler,
William Dilworth (oral history, Richmond, 2000)

CONTENTS

Early any weekday morning on the corners in Richmond, Virginia, where the number 16 bus can be caught, one very likely will see middle-aged to elderly (or at least so they appear) African American women waiting to take the next step of their trek to the far west end. The terminal point on that particular bus line is the entrance gate that leads into the University of Richmond campus. Few if any whites will be on this bus at that time on any day. But between five and seven P.M. on that same bus, on those same days, one will see an overwhelmingly white ridership of young to middle-aged white professionals returning home from downtown jobs. Some of them will be able to arrive at houses that had been cleaned by the black women day workers, modern-day domestics, who would most likely already have departed on buses going in the opposite direction.

Encounters in America—despite taking place in the same physical space and perhaps even on the same mode of transportation—seemingly always have been determined by matters of class and race. In a world where the oppressions of white supremacy, the privileges of class, and the subordination of women have cohered, enormous challenges are faced when one tries to disentangle and reconstruct the lives of and the relationships between the very rich and their servants. With extraordinary skill, vision, and dedication, historian Elizabeth O'Leary has brought into unprecedented focus the parallel but separate lives of Major James and Sallie May Dooley and their overwhelmingly African American and female staff.

The pages that follow provide a window through which to see individual male and female laborers who customarily are not seen. In breaking that tradition, the magnificent Maymont mansion ceases to tell a tale solely of its fabulously wealthy owners or the exquisite furnishings they acquired, parties they gave, or gardens they overlooked. It is also a work-place in which workers—black and white—labored diligently and with considerable skill. By following these individuals to their homes and to their communities, as well as by recounting their many steps each day at work, O'Leary has not only given us a refreshingly new view of the Gilded Age South. She has also shown us the transition from slavery to freedom and the way in which slave owners remade themselves—and were made into—employers of free black women and men. Theirs is a tale of fellow passengers traveling together but separately through America's past and, sometimes, its present.

Norrece T. Jones Jr.

This upstairs-downstairs study of Maymont House—presently open to the public as a Gilded Age house museum—had its first manifestation as a historic overview for a domestic-service exhibition and interpretation project. Its development is inseparable from that larger endeavor. With funding from the National Endowment for the Humanities alongside gifts from private individuals and foundations, Maymont Foundation has undertaken an ongoing, multiyear period of research, planning, and development. As funding permits, the mansion's service spaces are being carefully restored to their turn-of-the-century appearance and outfitted with period furnishings and artifacts. Visitors will soon be able to walk through the butler's pantry, basement entry hall, kitchen, food pantries, laundry, wine cellar, butler's bedroom, and maids' bedroom. They will also be able to explore a permanent exhibition about domestic service in Maymont House and the Gilded Age South.

As guest curator, I have had the fascinating task of finding and compiling evidence of the mansion's "invisible" workers of the past and finding ways to interpret their lives and labors to visitors and readers of today. In these efforts I have been the grateful beneficiary of the good work and generosity of many individuals. Over the past decade—and under the determined leadership of Dale Cyrus Wheary, Director of Historical Collections and Programs—a succession of museum personnel, scholars, and volunteers have found and organized the rare scraps of information about former Dooley employees. They began only with Sallie Dooley's will, with its handful of servant names, and a 1925 estate inventory that summed up the basement's contents with the single notation: "1 lot kitchen utensils— 50.00."

The effort to fill in the literal and figurative blank spaces gained momentum in 1992. The Maymont House Benevolent Society funded an extensive survey and documentation of the surviving physical features of the unrestored basement by historical architect Charles A. Phillips. Two years later, a grant from the William H. John G. Emma Scott Foundation supported new efforts to discover archival materials. Under the direction of Barbara Carson of the American Studies department at The College of William and Mary, a corps of scholars, students, and Maymont staff undertook a two-year search for extant primary documents, related civic and government records, and contemporary household literature. The team included Martha C. Vick, Barbara A. Curran, Carolyn E. Brucken, and Shannon Hughes. William E. Worthington Jr. produced an assessment of the mansion's household technology.

Anne Ferris Barger, former curatorial assistant, deserves special recognition for her research efforts and for establishing the initial project files. Other past and present Maymont Foundation staff members have researched aspects of the story, read drafts of the manuscript, and provided moral support along the way. They include Dotty Robinson, Carol Harris, Evelyn Zak, Liz Guarnieri, Elizabeth Terry, Kate Peeples, Terry Graham, and Mollie Malone. I particularly appreciate the volunteer assistance of Eva Brinkley, Thelma Robinson, and Robert Nelson. Research interns from area universities have lent a hand. They include Isabel Guajardo, Lynne George, Joseph Jackson, Matthew White, and Jeffrey Hamilton. A special thanks goes to Robin Hoffman, who provided steady assistance in the final push of research and fact checks.

No resource was more important to the project and to this study than the community at large. To date Maymont has sponsored five Community Roundtables, bringing together civic leaders; historians; church leaders; representatives from sister museums, universities, and archives; and friends and families of former domestic workers. These stimulating discussions have helped to shape interpretation and widen community networks and have prompted open, ongoing discourse about Maymont and Richmond's complex history.

In the course of research, the Maymont project staff gathered over fifty oral-history interviews with descendants and friends of former Dooley domestic employees, older Richmonders who worked in service, and people who grew up in elite homes in the early twentieth century. These firsthand remembrances lend incalculable resonance to the larger story. As interviewer for the majority of these oral histories, I remain deeply honored that these wonderful individuals sat down with me—often in their own living rooms—to share personal memories and candid insights. I am particularly grateful to Harold Bailey, Joseph Carter Jr., Mate Converse, Aubrey Fitzgerald, James Fitzgerald Jr., Maria Hoar, Audrey Smith, Mary Twiggs, Sylvester Walker, and Doris Woodson for patiently allowing me to return several times with "just one more question."

In this endeavor I have been also blessed with a generous circle of scholars and museum professionals who have variously advised, read, and edited portions of the manuscript. Norrece T. Jones Jr., the consummate professor who is both firm and kind, provided crucial critiques of the manuscript. At the same time Mary Tyler McClenahan graciously and judiciously reviewed final drafts of the text. Mary Lynn Bayliss, who serves as Maymont's intrepid volunteer historian, has shared her files and insights about the Dooleys and their times. Her steady research has helped to build an important compendium of Dooley-related documents at Maymont House over the past decade. Furthermore, there is no way to repay the gifts of time and expertise offered by Bruce Berryhill, Barbara Carson, David Park Curry, Gregg Kimball, Curtis Lyons, Ed Peeples, Susan Rawles, Benjamin Ross, Barbara Ryan, Emily Salmon, and Leni Sorensen. I especially appreciate the steady counsel of Lauranett Lee, who also interviewed some of the oral-history subjects for the project. The staff of the Valentine Museum/Richmond History Center—in particular the imperturbable and adept Teresa Roane—has provided essential assistance in the compilation of historical data and images.

The domestic-service project benefits from long-standing friend and patron Sally Todd, who has been particularly generous with funding, artifacts, memories, and her constant, affirming support. A grant from the Robins Foundation supported the compilation of videotaped oral-history interviews. Other sponsors include Merle D. Martin, Sue Miller, James Emerson Tashjian-Brown, and the Anne Carter Robins and Walter R. Robins Jr. Foundation.

I dare say that there would no be exhibition, educational programs, or book about Maymont's domestic workers without the leadership of Dale Wheary. Maintaining the vision of interpreting the history of *all* the people of Maymont House, she has been an invaluable colleague. Geoffrey Platt Jr., Maymont Foundation's Executive Director, has proven both encouraging and supportive over the past four years.

I appreciate the professional and supportive staff who worked with me at the University of Virginia Press, including Ellen Satrom, managing editor, and Martha Farlow, design production manager, as well as Sarah Nestor, copy editor. Boyd Zenner, my acquisitions editor at the press, proved an especially effective shepherd with her ongoing enthusiasm and sound, calm advice.

Last but far from least, I am grateful to my friends and family, who kindly and with glazed eyes listened to the triumphs or frustrations of each day's paper chase. And, always and forever, I thank my husband, John Martin, for his ongoing good humor, patience, and love.

Acknowl-
edgments

———

FROM MORNING TO NIGHT

allie May Dooley had summoned her cook from Maymont's basement kitchen. She waited in the pink drawing room in anticipation of the sound of the swinging door to the dining room and the crackle of Frances Walker's starched uniform. Smoothing her own black taffeta gown, she seated herself on a gilded side chair and reflected on her duties as mistress of Maymont. From her mother and grandmother, she had learned to direct black servants in a kind but firm manner. Of course in her youth they had been slaves. But she and her husband, James Dooley, had managed the transition to having waged labor in their service in the post–Civil War years. After fifty years of directing her own house—and in truth, as Major Dooley's fortunes grew, so did the size and contents of their residences—she still took pride in the smooth running of the domestic mill.

Now in her seventies and newly widowed, she had turned over supervisory tasks to her niece, Florence Elder, who had come to live at Maymont in recent years. Florence was a great comfort to the childless couple, and she had learned well how to set the menus and direct the house staff of eight. But Sallie Dooley remained vigilant. This afternoon, for instance, she had caught a glimpse of an unfamiliar black girl walking down the service lane. Drawing closer to the window, she watched the child approach the house and disappear down the stairs to the servants' basement entrance.

Quick steps carried Mrs. Dooley to the speaking tube on the wall in the butler's pantry. Its sharp whistle called the cook to the other end below stairs.

"Yes, ma'am?"

"Frances, who was that girl who came in just now?"

"That's my niece, Missus Dooley. She's here for a spell. Virgie's real mannerly and quiet. She won't be in the way."

"I'd like to see her. Bring her up, please."

Glancing at the large kitchen's wall clock, Frances Twiggs Walker was satisfied with the afternoon's work. She made a mental inventory of the progress toward the evening meal. The yeast bread was rising nicely; under the huck toweling, it made a satisfying bulge in the yellow bowl. The green beans had been snapped, the apples peeled. Her grown daughter, Hannah, working as second cook, was dutifully checking the hens for stray quills after plucking.

At age sixty, Frances Walker had reached the top of her profession. Having honed her skills as a live-in cook in other wealthy households, she had accepted the job at Maymont four years earlier in 1919. She could do plain cooking—quick breads, stews, and pies—that suited the Virginian taste of everyone in the house, both upstairs and down. Mrs. Walker's reputation, however, was made on the elaborate French dishes that her ladies required for luncheons and dinner parties.

When young Virgie made her entrance into the kitchen, Mrs. Walker gave the child a quick hug. Returning to the tasks at hand, she reflected that her brother, Willie, had raised a sweet girl. But there were eight children coming up in that house. To ease the economic strain, her aunt had agreed to keep and feed Virgie on occasional weekends. That her employer didn't know of the arrangement caused her little concern. The few bites of food seemed inconsequential in this house of plenty, and there was room in her big bed at night. Other than the chauffeurs—one being her son Joseph—few noticed the small visitor to her rooms over the garage.

Through a second generation after slave times, the Twiggs family of Caroline County generally kept its boys in the country to farm and learn carpentry skills. If the girls didn't marry and stay in Ruther Glen, the elders managed to send them the thirty miles to Richmond for schooling and to find work in the white folks' houses. It took coordinated efforts on the part of the extended family. During the week, for example, young Virgie Twiggs lived with her mother's brother and his wife on Marshall Street in Jackson Ward. Some Fridays, like today, she rode the streetcar into the suburbs, stopping near the gates of the sprawling Maymont estate. The ten-minute walk down the service lane brought her past the garage. From Aunt Frances's bedroom upstairs, she enjoyed watching the Dooleys' sleek motorcars come and go. At this time of day, however, she knew to find her aunt in the basement of the big stone house with its towers and stained-glass windows.

Settling at the kitchen table with schoolbooks and her doll, she stayed well out of the way of her aunt and cousin. She loved to watch them bustling about in their gray uniforms and big white aprons. Both had straight black hair that gave witness to their mixed black and Indian heritage. From earlier visits Virgie had grown accustomed to the ringing bell of the basement's call box, with its arrows that pointed to numbers for the rooms upstairs. And she knew the whistle of the speaking tube and the buzzing murmur of a voice on the other end. Usually, it was Mr. Dilworth, the butler; on rare occasions it was Mrs. Dooley herself. Today, with a serious face, her aunt informed her that Mrs. Dooley wanted to see *her*.

As Virgie stood before Sallie Dooley, she leaned slightly toward the reassuring presence of her aunt. The previous minutes melted into a blur of impressions: pats and tugs of hasty grooming, the rhythmic sound of their footsteps on the narrow oak treads of the back stairs, the hushed glide across thick carpets, and moving glimmers of light reflecting off porcelain, silver, and the pearls around the throat of her aunt's employer. Earlier, Virgie had only observed Mrs. Dooley from a distance, watching her descend the steps of the mansion's porte cochere to be handed into the back seat of the Pierce-Arrow. Now, with large eyes, the child could take in every aspect of the woman's face, hair, hands, and dress.

After introductions and a solemn handshake, Virgie answered questions about her age, parents, and progress in school. Bending a bit closer, the elderly woman added with a smile, "Now, you have a nice visit with your aunt. Then you go straight home, you hear?"

"Yes, ma'am." Virgie looked up into her aunt's face, which revealed nothing.

Mrs. Dooley spoke again. "I hope, young lady, that when you grow up, you'll be a fine cook like your aunt."

Laying hands on her niece's shoulders, Frances Walker leaned forward to respond; "Thank you, ma'am, but I don't want her to be a cook." Meeting eyes and offering polite nods, employer and employee recognized that the interview had come to an end.

Downstairs, Virgie wanted to ask many questions. They could talk later, Aunt Frances told her, once they had walked to the garage in the darkness of night, climbed the stairs, turned out the light, and snuggled down in bed.

Today, when guests enter the front hall of Maymont House, they often experience a sense of wonder similar to that of visitors who called on James Henry and Sallie May Dooley a century ago. Still in place within the walls of this grand country house are many of the couple's opulent furnishings and objets d'art. As in their own time, the mansion and its contents testify to the tastes and lifestyle of the Virginia multimillionaire and his wife who built, decorated, and lived at Maymont between 1893 and 1925. Less evident are reminders of other individuals whose labors once sustained the residence's order and beauty. Call buttons, a butler's pantry, a dumbwaiter, and a narrow back stairway remain. Below stairs, a labyrinth of unadorned, whitewashed rooms still attests to an earlier use as work and living spaces for Maymont's domestic servants.[1]

When the Dooleys died within a few years of each other in the mid-1920s, they bequeathed their wealth to various charitable causes. They also gave Maymont to the city of Richmond, the estate serving since as public park and historic house museum. In the 1970s it came under the auspices of the private, nonprofit Maymont Foundation and was listed on the National Register of Historic Places. Today, visitors can not only explore the restored mansion, gardens, and ornamental grounds; they can also enjoy added attractions including an interactive Nature Center, a Children's Farm, outdoor wildlife exhibitions, and a historic carriage collection.

Maymont House opened to the public as a house museum nearly eighty years ago. Its interpretive focus has rested primarily on the history of its prosperous owners and the splendor of their Gilded Age showplace. Equally compelling, however, are the lesser-known stories of the men and women who once experienced Maymont as a workplace. It is difficult at best to craft a historical "snapshot" of Maymont's domestic work and workers. At the presumed directive of Sallie Dooley, the couple's personal papers and household accounts were destroyed following her death in 1925.[2] Enough material survives, however, to help reconstruct aspects of Maymont's social, economic, architectural, and technological systems. Correspondence and financial documents discovered in outside repositories—including the Dooley papers in the Branch and Company records at the Virginia Historical Society—provide important details. Governmental statistics and surveys help establish a demographic base. Contemporary literature—nonfiction, including cookbooks and household manuals, and fiction, such as Sallie Dooley's own novel, *Dem Good Ole Times*—gives some indication of prevailing notions and practices of domestic management and service in upper-class households. In our own era, the determination of scholars of "new history" to document the experiences of people of color, women, and the working class in America has resulted in a widening contextual foundation. And recent architectural and technological surveys of Maymont House itself offer invaluable information about extant features and site-specific clues to residential systems long vanished.

The most compelling insights, however, come from oral-history interviews with descendants and friends of former Maymont employees—including Virgie Twiggs Payne, on whose remembrances the prologue is based.[3] Additional oral histories were gathered from Dooley descendants, as well as from older Richmonders who either worked in domestic service or grew up in upper-class households staffed with servants. These diverse voices bring resonance and texture to the larger story.

During their residency at Maymont, the Dooleys typically employed seven to ten individuals to serve in the positions of butler, second butler, cook, kitchen maid, housemaid, lady's maid, driver (coachman and chauffeur), and laundress. An estate manager and about twenty additional workers were employed to maintain the grounds of the one-hundred-acre estate and work in the stables and garage.[4] Of the household staff, some employees worked full-time, others part-time; extra workers were hired weekly or as needed. A few resided in the house or on the estate, but most "lived out"—that is, they returned to their separate homes and families during off-duty hours. Workers ranged in age from their late teens to mid-sixties; most were single, but several were married with children. While, historically, women far outnumbered men in American service demographics, menservants figured prominently at Maymont. Of the twenty-five identified employees during the Dooleys' tenure, eleven are male. Four became World War I veterans. Little information remains to indicate the educational level of Maymont's domestic staff, though census records indicate a high literacy rate among those workers listed. Nor do we know whether any received formal training; it is likely that most staff members learned from on-the-job experience.

With few exceptions, the Maymont workers were African American.[5] German-born Emily Lackmiok, listed as "servant" in the 1900 census, is the only immigrant employee known to have been retained by the Dooleys. At least one coachman and two of the Maymont chauffeurs were white males. Census returns indicate that most staff members were Virginia born, although a handful were native midwesterners who had migrated to Richmond sometime previously. Most of the staff was drawn from the greater Richmond area, with several employees residing in the immediate neighborhood of the estate.

The Dooleys' way of recruiting their household workers remains an object of speculation. Newspaper advertisements, employment agencies, and word of mouth were the traditional methods of the day. It is likely that Maymont staff members were located primarily through personal contacts, kinship ties providing an important resource. In the 1920s, for example, six grown children of Maymont's head cook, Frances Twiggs Walker, came on staff—including her daughter of the same name. In the same decade the Dooleys employed Georgia Anderson as lady's maid and her brother James Lewis as yardman and occasional driver.

The enticement of competent workers from other households also took place, though it was considered bad form among friends. Sallie Dooley likely sampled Frances Walker's culinary skills when dining in the home of William R. and Catherine Cox. A few years and employers later, the experienced Mrs. Walker took the position of head cook at Maymont. An undated letter also documents friendly bargaining between Sallie Dooley and an acquaintance over the services of an unnamed domestic.

Kate Logan of Algoma, in Howardsville, Virginia, wrote of her discovery that Mrs. Dooley had asked her maid to come to work at Maymont by the end of the week. Surprised but conceding that the arrangement was convenient to her own staffing needs, Mrs. Logan proposed sharing the employee: "She has been pretty well trained and is a good girl. I have had her for years, and I was glad to hear she was going to you. As she comes back to me in the summer and you are away during that season, I think it will suit you also. She can go at any time now."[6]

The recruitment and supervision of Maymont's domestic employees were the province of Sallie Dooley, following prescribed gender roles of the era. James Dooley likely played a role, however, in recruiting and supervising the estate managers for Maymont and Swannanoa. He would also have selected his coachmen and chauffeurs. Two chauffeur-mechanics—brothers James and C. Hamilton Fitzgerald—came from Waynesboro near Swannanoa, the Dooleys' summer home in the Blue Ridge Mountains. Dooley may also have had a hand in locating and hiring grounds workers, assisted no doubt by Louis Taliaferro, Maymont's longtime estate manager.

For over twenty-five years, Louis Taliaferro (pronounced "Toliver") oversaw the upkeep of Maymont's sizable grounds. Coming to work for the Dooleys in 1899 when he was only nineteen, he eventually resided at the gatehouse, where he and his wife maintained a small garden and some livestock. Taliaferro—listed in census records as a Virginia-born white man—described himself as a trusted employee and the only nonfamily member who had the combination to the house safe. In their wills, the Dooleys made arrangements that allowed Louis Taliaferro to maintain his role as overseer and to reside on the estate for the remainder of his life.[7]

As the Dooleys grew older, the childless couple invited an unmarried niece, Florence Elder, to reside with them. The daughter of Sallie Dooley's older sister, Anna, Miss Elder relocated from Staunton sometime after 1904 and remained at Maymont until 1925, when she helped oversee the transition of the estate's ownership to the city of Richmond following her aunt's death. During her residency, she served as a companion to Mrs. Dooley and increasingly assisted in managing the household staff and accounts. Records indicate that in addition to room and board, Florence

Elder occasionally received an allowance. As her widowed aunt became infirm, she assumed more responsibility, especially when the household relocated to Swannanoa for the summer. A reluctant bookkeeper, she wrote to the family business manager in Richmond, "I am keeping a strict account of all money . . . and will be more than glad to turn it all over to you this fall. I don't believe there was anybody in the world who hates to handle other people's money as I do!"[8] A close family member who affectionately referred to the Dooleys as "Aunt Sallie" and "Uncle Jim," Florence Elder would not have been perceived as a member of the domestic staff but as her aunt's supervising agent.

For thirty-five years Maymont House witnessed the dynamic interplay between employer and employee, upper-class and working-class individuals, white and black. This nexus was played out against the backdrop of rapidly changing domestic technology. It was also set in the changing social and political landscape of a segregated South. During the Maymont era, social and political limitations imposed on black southerners by the dominant white culture systematically hardened into Jim Crow laws. Maymont's domestic staff of 1925 consequently had far fewer civil and social liberties than did their predecessors of 1893.

Sharing domestic realms did not mean that employer and worker shared experiences and viewpoints. James and Sallie Dooley sought out, hired, and depended on numerous household employees to maintain their lavish residences and lifestyle. To meet business, political, and social obligations with the assurance and elegance deemed appropriate to their standing among Richmond's white, moneyed elite, they relied on a domestic staff competent in both ordinary and specialized tasks. In turn, numerous individuals—predominantly black and many whose names are unknown today—depended on their jobs at Maymont for a livelihood. Under scrutiny and sometimes difficult conditions, staff members met the day-to-day challenges of running an elaborate household. Behind the scenes, they maintained the thirty-three-room mansion, fed seven to twelve people on a daily basis and hundreds on occasion, washed and ironed clothes and linens, helped the Dooleys bathe and dress, and transported them in well-running carriages and motorcars.

Little remains to testify to the kinds of relationships that developed between the Dooleys and the men and women in their employ. Physical evidence tells us that the couple provided their staff with adequate work and living space in the mansion. Written documentation shows that, by the standards of their time and socioeconomic station, the couple paid their employees above-average wages and, following Mrs. Dooley's death, left staff bequests amounting to thousands of dollars. Oral history also offers evidence of the cordial regard some employees held toward the Dooleys.[9] At the same time, there were no longtime "retainers," as heralded in other households and in the literature of the day. Census and city-directory listings indicate that the longest employment period for a Maymont staff member is five to six years—a tenure that is nonetheless beyond the three to eighteen months of most domestic workers of the period.[10]

What follows is a two-part consideration of the separate but parallel experiences of server and served at Maymont House. "The View from the Drawing Room" introduces James and Sallie Dooley and particulars of their opulent domain and social milieu; "The View from the Kitchen" presents the lives and labors of the household employees, both within and beyond the boundaries of the estate. These sections are followed by biographical profiles of Dooley employees from 1880 to 1925.

While we cannot wholly reconstruct the experiences of the Dooleys and their several employees, by examining various historic resources and personal narratives together we might catch a glimpse of the former inhabitants of Maymont, both above and below stairs. These overlapping experiences and often-divergent perspectives contribute to our larger understanding of Gilded Age Richmond, the South, and the United States.[11]

Throughout their lives, James and Sallie Dooley were attended by African American servants—first slaves, then paid employees. As young adults in post–Civil War Virginia, they witnessed the transformation of the master/mistress-slave relationship to that of employer-employee. In subsequent decades, they further experienced and negotiated the evolving dynamics of that work relationship. While embracing the progressive business impulses of the New South, the Dooleys, like most of their contemporaries, maintained their identities as traditional southerners. Vivid memories of the Old South's slave system likely shaped their preferences and practices as employers. At the same time the couple was part of America's Gilded Age elite, whose elaborate lifestyles and large residences required sizable domestic staffs. Educated, well-traveled, and well-read, the Dooleys were cognizant of changing upper-class tastes in fashion, manners, social mores, and approaches to household management.

Childhood Traditions and Influences

James H. Dooley was born in 1841 and grew up in the upper-middle-class urban household of his parents, John and Sarah Dooley. His father had emigrated from Ireland well before the massive influx of impoverished emigrants fled the ravages of their homeland's famine at midcentury. Within a decade of his arrival in Richmond about 1836, the elder Dooley established himself as a prominent citizen. Though never achieving the kind of vast fortune his son would later accrue, John Dooley Sr. made a substantial income between 1840 and 1860 as a hat manufacturer, furrier, and merchant. By 1860 he owned four adult slaves—three females and a male—to see to the needs of his family, which included son James, then nineteen.[1]

Dooley and his sons, James and John, fought in the Confederate Army during the Civil War. All three men were tended by a young slave, Ned Haines, during separate campaigns with the First Virginia Regiment. Described in the younger John Dooley's diary as "our black servant boy," Haines traveled alongside each of them during long infantry marches, slept at their sides, and functioned as body servant and personal courier for supplies and food. On separate occasions—when brothers James, in 1862, and then John, in 1863, were wounded and captured by Union troops—Ned Haines made his way back to Richmond. James Dooley, a private who later carried the honorific title of Major, sustained a lifelong disability from battle wounds.[2]

The "unfortunate War Between the States," as he later described it, interrupted James Dooley's academic pursuits. Just before its commencement, he earned an A.B. degree in "moral philosophy" from Georgetown College in Washington, D.C. Immediately following the war's end in 1865, he returned to his alma mater to complete an A.M. He also began to read law at a prominent Richmond firm at this time. In a short while the new attorney established a practice and was keeping a sharp eye out for promising investments. This interest in accumulating wealth was not a new obsession. Many years earlier, a fourteen-year-old James had inscribed in his Latin dictionary: "When I have $5,178,360 I will stop making money. J. D."[3] By the century's end, he had retired from the law and was closing in on his childhood dream of multimillions. In census and city-directory listings of the late nineteenth century, Dooley's occupation was consistently listed as "lawyer" or "attorney at law." After 1900 a new designation made its appearance: "capitalist."[4]

Unlike her future husband, who was first generation Irish American, Sarah O. "Sallie" May was descended from some of Virginia's oldest English families, numbering among her ancestors Edward Digges, governor of Virginia, 1655–58.[5] She was the eighth of nine children born to Henry and Julia Jones May of Lunenburg County, Virginia. Her father was a prominent country physician whose office sat very close to Lunenburg County Courthouse. This central location afforded the doctor access to patients all over Southside Virginia. It is not clear whether the May family resided at the same site as the medical office or lived two miles south at

Locust Grove, the large plantation belonging to Mrs. May's parents, Peter and Sally Bacon Jones—and the location of Sallie's birth in 1846.[6]

Government records give some indication of the configuration of Sallie May's childhood home. The 1850 census—enumerating white residents only—lists family members (including four-year-old Sallie) along with a twenty-year-old, Virginia-born male carpenter and a twenty-five-year-old female from Massachusetts.[7] For the same year, county records list twenty-two African Americans above the age of twelve as taxable property belonging to her father, Henry May. Housekeeping and child-care needs were great in the large May family, and it is likely that several of these slaves worked as house servants. From their earliest years, Sallie May and her siblings would have learned from their elders how to direct black subordinates to meet personal and household needs.[8]

As a family, the Mays were tied closely through kinship, custom, and politics to one of the most uncompromising proslavery contingencies of the commonwealth. Going back at least three generations, Sallie May's ancestors were members of Lunenburg County's prosperous planter class. Tax and court records indicate that her great-grandfather Peter Jones owned hundreds of acres along Reedy Creek (on which Locust Grove once stood) and more than twenty slaves. Inheriting both land and slaves, her maternal grandfather, also named Peter Jones, expanded the family property. By 1815 he owned more than two thousand acres and forty slaves—holdings exceeding those of most other planters in the county.[9]

Lunenburg County—which was and still is agricultural—grew wealthy in the first half of the nineteenth century through tobacco crops. Heavy production required an expanding slave-labor force, whose numbers made up two-thirds of the county's total population at midcentury. Planter families like the Joneses were heavily invested in an economic system based on slavery. Nevertheless, Sallie May's uncle, Benjamin Harrison May, emancipated a slave named Gensey Snow in 1825 for "extraordinary merit in nursing other slaves during an epidemic." Changing her name to Jane Minor, she saved her nursing wages over the following three decades in order to purchase the freedom of sixteen slaves in the Petersburg area.[10]

On the eve of the Civil War, Lunenburg planter families rallied squarely behind the Confederate cause. As a teenager, Sallie May would have heard partisan arguments by Southside politicians—including her cousin David Stokes, who presided over a committee of Lunenburg citizens advocating immediate secession from the Union on grounds of states' rights and in defense of the slave system.[11] Earlier, southsider James Gholson of neighboring Brunswick County voiced a prevailing argument against abolition:

> The Slaves of Virginia are as happy a laboring class as exists upon the habitable earth. They are as well fed, well clothed and as well treated. In health, but reasonable labour is required of them—in sickness, they are nursed and attended to. In times of plenty, they live in waste—in times of scarcity, they do not want—they are content to-day, and have no care or anxiety for to-morrow. Cruel treatment of them is discountenanced by society, and until of late, their privileges were daily extending. Among what labouring class will you find more happiness and less misery? Not among the serfs and laboring poor of Europe! No, Sir.—Nor among the servants to the North of us.[12]

Gholson articulated the region's prevailing rationale that slavery benefited and protected African Americans, who were perceived as helpless and dependent. In the early twentieth century, this antebellum notion of benevolent slaveholding would resonate in Sallie Dooley's own writing, *Dem Good Ole Times* (1906).

Setting Up Housekeeping in the Postwar South

James and Sallie May Dooley began their married life together in 1869 in a South dramatically altered after four years of Civil War. Richmond had suffered physical and economic ruin, sending businessmen like John Dooley into financial upheaval. When the elder Dooley died suddenly in 1868, James took on the responsibilities of managing his father's estate, caring for his invalid mother and—the following year—acquiring a wife. After marrying Sallie May in Staunton, Virginia, where she was visiting older sisters, James Dooley brought her to Richmond during the height of Reconstruction.[13]

In the aftermath of defeat, the economy of the Confederacy's fallen capital was devastated. Commerce had been disrupted when the evacuation fire and rampant looting at war's end damaged a large portion of the city's business district—including the hat store of John Dooley Sr. In order to receive food rations from the occupying Federal army, Richmonders had to swear an oath of allegiance to the United States Constitution and its government and accept the abolishment of slavery. As a new attorney and notary public, James Dooley was called on to witness such affidavits of allegiance.[14]

The city's African American community was in flux as individuals sorted out families and tried to locate sources of paid labor. Thousands of refugees from the surrounding countryside came into Richmond in search of food, shelter, medical care, and work. They joined a large population of urban blacks already in place, including many house servants who had left their former owners after emancipation. With support systems formed through extended family, churches, and a growing number of secret societies, black residents established themselves in Richmond. Many found positions in tobacco, flour, and iron factories; others located jobs as waged domestic workers. Still others remained as house servants with their original owners, though, as the *Richmond Dispatch* conceded, "there is no realization of their freedom while they remain in the service of the same persons." During the same period, white householders began anew, assessing staffing needs despite their depleted finances.[15]

Compared to the privileged lifestyle of their youth, James and Sallie's married life began under more modest circumstances. Newlyweds in their mid-twenties, they chose to live in a boarding residence that had its own domestic staff. Boarding—a common arrangement for young families in American cities throughout the nineteenth century—relieved wives of the burden of supervising meal preparation and housekeeping. Among boarding houses, the range of accommodations, furnishings, meals, and service varied from austere to elaborate.[16]

The year 1881 established the Dooleys in an independent household at 212 West Franklin, Richmond's most stylish street. West Franklin featured a combination of new mansions alongside older historical structures. The Dooleys' residence, built about 1807, was in the latter category. In 1886 the *Richmond State* listed it among "The Finest Residences" of Richmond.

"Elegant and comfortable," the mansion had an exceptional library, "the fitting up of which is said to have cost $3,000." The couple's living arrangements at this fashionable address no doubt conveyed the growing prosperity of one of Richmond's most reputable lawyers, politicians, and businessmen. In their Franklin Street home, the Dooleys retained a household staff. The 1885–86 *Chataigne's Directory of Richmond* lists two African American men in residence: Fleming Jones, butler, and Joseph Claiborne, driver. Employees who lived out, whose names were not recorded, would have held other positions such as those of cook, maid, and laundress. Unfortunately, federal census records for 1890 do not survive to indicate the configuration of the household five years later. The city directory, however, indicates that Joseph Claiborne continued his position with the Dooleys at Franklin Street until 1892.[17]

James Dooley, having steadily recovered from the upheaval of the Civil War, parlayed his intelligence, capital, and luck into a substantial fortune during the 1880s and 1890s. Through his law practice, business investments, railroads, and real estate—and with Sallie May at his side—he entered the highest of America's socioeconomic ranks during the last quarter of the century. In 1892 the *Tribune Monthly* listed 4,047 millionaires in the United States; James H. Dooley was among them.[18] As their affluence grew, the couple's living standards and household needs increased accordingly.

In 1886 James Dooley purchased a dairy farm in Henrico County, along the north bank of the James River and two miles from the center of Richmond. In a short time he named the suburban property "May-Mont" in honor of his wife, Sallie May, and registered it in her name. After several years of development and construction, the grand mansion and the surrounding estate were ready for occupancy in 1893. The couple's move to Maymont that year heralded their arrival into the upper echelon of America's moneyed elite. The stylish new residence and ornamental grounds were the most visible signs of the Dooleys' expanding fortunes. The fact that they could retain a large, specialized domestic staff was another.[19]

Domestic Arrangements in Maymont House

The architectural elements of Maymont House, inside and out, have survived fairly intact over the century since the Dooleys first took up residency. Designed by Edgerton Rogers in the late 1880s, the three-storied mansion exhibits a synthesis of the picturesque characteristics of Romanesque Revival and Queen Anne—two prominent styles favored by the newly affluent in America's Gilded Age. The mansion still retains the original configuration of work and living spaces for the Dooleys and their sizable domestic staff. Its layout also reveals prevailing design standards that separate private and public realms, family and service spaces.[20]

For those Americans whose financial resources increased in the last quarter of the century, single-family dwellings grew in size and complexity. Large entrance halls became transitional areas in which servants mediated between families and visitors. At the same time pantries, back corridors, and stairs provided buffer zones between server and served.[21] Employers were not to be burdened with the sounds, sights, or smells of household chores. As historian Faye Dudden points out, "changing domestic architecture reflected the sense that domestics should inhabit areas of the home where all the work was to be performed, while the family lived in other areas designed for display, comfort, intimacy, even study, but not housework."[22]

Employees, unless performing such ceremonial tasks as waiting at table or answering the door, were to be unobtrusive if not invisible. As a household manual of the period explains: "No well-ordered house has noisy servants. The housekeeping in every department should move like perfect, well-oiled machinery with invisible wheels. Shrieks of laughter from the kitchen, singing and calling through the halls, stamp a house at once as belonging to the vulgar and uncultivated. Let the comforts and luxuries provided for your family and guests come to them as by magic."[23]

Until given permission or instructions to enter family spaces—literally called "on the carpet"—servants were required to remain in specific residential precincts and to make use of back entrances, halls, stairs, and rooms. Audrey Smith, daughter of Sallie Dooley's personal maid, Georgia Anderson, observed that staff members understood residential boundaries. "You did clean the house," she noted, "but you did not have accessibility to the house. You came in at the basement end.... The very fact that you had designated exits and entrances lets you know that the house is under the authority of the Madam. When something had to be done, *she* would come to *you*—or ask you to come into the library. That was a fore-gone thing."[24]

At Maymont House, the space allocated for service purposes is sig-nificant, accounting for a third of all the rooms in the mansion. The ar-chitectural arrangement conforms to the layout of most middle- and upper-class urban residences of the era. The basement—entered outside through a subterranean door on the house's east facade or inside by ele-vator and by the back service stairway—comprises a series of work, stor-age, and living spaces grouped around a central furnace room. This lower level includes the kitchen, laundry, and drying closet. It also holds stor-age rooms for foods, wine, and coal. Moreover, the basement houses resi-dential and rest spaces for employees: an area for staff dining in the kitchen, a lavatory consisting of a single toilet, the butler's bedroom, and, in the opposite corner, dormitory space for female servants. The first floor of Maymont House includes the butler's pantry with an adjacent storage room. The third floor houses a housekeeper's room and a servants' bath-room with toilet, sink, and tub.[25] Aboveground, the service rooms and stairs are oriented to the southeast corner of the house.

Below stairs Maymont's service spaces are fairly spacious, with nine-foot ceilings. Furnished throughout with combination gas-electric light fixtures, many of the basement rooms have full-length windows. Exte-rior areaways along the east and west foundations allow sunlight to pene-trate and air to circulate through this system of large windows. Paint analy-sis reveals that during the Dooley era the walls were painted white; the wood trim was initially painted shades of brown (1893) and then two shades of green (ca. 1910). Virginia Alexander, who visited Maymont as a child in the 1920s, remembered the basement as "nice and clean."[26]

The mansion's basement was equipped and finished at a rather mod-est level compared to what was available for an upper-class household of the era. The lack of wall and floor tiles in the kitchen—a prominent fea-ture in contemporary household manuals and magazines—suggests that there may have been some cost cutting during the final year of construc-tion in 1893.[27] Nevertheless, the service spaces are arranged and equipped to meet prevailing upper-middle-class standards. The design and layout for the employees' work and living spaces are no-nonsense, utilitarian rooms in which workers maintained the mansion's heating system, stored cleaning implements and supplies, and prepared food and washed and ironed laundry. A dumbwaiter, annunciator (call) box, speaking tube, stairway, and elevator linked the realms of employer and employee.

Technological Advances

Across the decades of their long lives, the Dooleys witnessed dramatic changes in household technology. As children brought up in separate city and country environments, James and Sallie would have experienced domestic systems at differing stages of advancement. At midcentury young James resided in an urban home likely heated by coal burned in iron fire grates, ate food purchased at the market and prepared on a wood- or coal-burning cookstove, and wore garments handmade by a local tailor or machine made, purchased from a merchandise store. His parents' Broad Street residence would have been transformed by gas lighting in the 1850s, fueled by the city's coal-gas plant.[28] As a male, James would have had few if any responsibilities in housecleaning tasks, cooking, and clothing care. These would have been accomplished by house slaves, supervised and assisted in varying degrees by his mother and sisters.

In rural Lunenburg County, Sallie May might have spent her earliest years in a house where heat was still produced from and meals prepared over open fireplaces. Wood- and coal-burning stoves were likely introduced for both functions during her childhood. Foodstuffs came from her parents' own crops and livestock, supplemented by goods provided, purchased, and bartered from neighbors and family. Meals were the culmination of long hours of harvesting, butchering, preserving, cooking, milling, and baking. Household lighting came from oil lamps and candles. As the daughter of a physician, Sallie may have owned some special articles of clothing acquired from stores in larger towns like Petersburg or Richmond. More typically, however, the Mays would have purchased fabric and relied on local seamstresses, perhaps including one of their slaves, to produce garments.[29] It is difficult to know the extent that Sallie, her mother, and her sisters participated in cooking, cleaning, and sewing tasks. With skilled slave servants, they may have limited their contributions to special baked goods and dishes and "fancy" needlework such as embroidery.

In the childhood homes of both James and Sallie, water from outdoor wells and attendance to daily necessities were accomplished with bowls and pitchers, chamber pots, and outdoor privies. Their clothing and linens, laundered by house slaves, were washed by hand in large tubs, dried on outdoor lines, and pressed with flatirons heated on a stove.[30]

The late nineteenth century brought dramatic technological changes in household systems, particularly in America's upper-class homes. The introduction of electricity, central-heating systems, and internal plumbing with hot and cold running water and flush commodes brought levels of domestic comfort unimagined by earlier generations. Ready-made clothing from department stores and catalogs, commercially processed foods, grocery stores, bakeries, and commercial steam laundries helped the American domestic economy shift from production to consumption.[31]

When planning the design of Maymont House, the Dooleys took some advantage of current residential technology. The mansion was installed with a boiler-fed central heating system, gas and electrical lighting, telephones, an electric elevator, indoor plumbing with hot and cold running water, two lavatories, and three full bathrooms that each included a tub, sink, and toilet. Very few documents and artifacts remain to help us form a definitive inventory of household appliances in the service spaces. With rapid technological advances in the early decades of the twentieth century, the mansion's early icebox, washtub, brooms, and flatirons could have been replaced systematically—and as needed—by an electric refrigerator, washing machine, vacuum cleaner, and electric irons. The lack of wall outlets in the basement, however, gives strong evidence that technology remained static downstairs over the thirty-five-year period.[32] Several repair receipts from the 1920s locate a then-unreliable Majestic range in the Maymont kitchen. The old coal-burning stove may have been original to the house, surviving over time with regular maintenance.[33] It was still in place at the time of Mrs. Dooley's death in 1925, as was, no doubt, a three-decade-long accumulation of assorted equipment. Swannanoa, the Dooley's summer residence in the Blue Ridge Mountains, was outfitted with more up-to-date contrivances. The fact that the Dooleys approved the installation of a central-vacuum system at their summer home in 1912 suggests some interest on their part—or that of their architect—in new residential technology. Eight years later, Swannanoa estate manager G. G. Dalhouse wrote to ask: "Have you ever thought any more about putting an electric range at your house? I have a cousin who has used one and she says they are grand things to have." The Dooleys conceded; a new range was in the Swannanoa kitchen by July 1920.[34]

Overall, it was not until the 1920s that advanced household technology became widespread in the United States. Even then, development lagged behind in the South. Oral histories indicate that contemporary upper-class households in Richmond were still typically furnished with coal-burning stoves and ice-cooled refrigerators instead of electric appliances. Employers tended to focus on the end results of chores—well-cooked meals, clean rooms, fresh laundry—not the hours or effort these entailed. As long as the results were satisfactory above stairs, it appears that the old ways and means remained standard below stairs. Whether or not Maymont included progressive inventions on the domestic front, workers there utilized equipment and systems that had yet to reach many middle-class and most working-class homes. On duty, the mansion staff was relieved of such traditional chores as carrying water in from outside or the daily chopping of wood for cooking and heating—tasks that most still performed in their own homes.[35]

In affluent residences such as Maymont, laborsaving devices would have eliminated some of the drudgery of housework. As historian Ruth Cowan points out, however, they did not eliminate the amount of labor, as the period also ushered in more complex standards of entertaining, cooking, and cleaning.[36]

Gilded Age Grandeur and Requirements of Service

The Maymont era brought widening prosperity and an increasing demand for domestic workers in middle- and upper-class homes nationwide. As one scholar notes, "Americans reached the zenith of their craving for servants during the Gilded Age." This desire was fueled by the ongoing need of homemakers for assistance with the heavier tasks of cleaning, cooking, laundering, and child care. At the end of the nineteenth century, household chores became even more complicated with increasing standards of hygiene and changing technology and equipment. Alongside such practical necessities, the growing demand for servants was also driven by an expanding desire for material abundance, signs of status, and adherence to elaborate social ritual.[37]

The Gilded Age was known, even at the time, for an unprecedented display of personal fortunes. Wealth, Thorstein Veblen argued in *The Theory of the Leisure Class* (1899), became a standard criterion for respectability in American society and the model of reputability for an aspiring middle class. Coining his now-famous catch phrases "conspicuous leisure" and "conspicuous consumption," the economist noted the propensity among affluent Americans for acquiring and showing the "latest properties of dress, furniture and equipage." In Veblen's assessment, servants figured prominently in such display—not only as costly household expenditures but also as outward symbols of a family's ascension in social and economic position. Present-day historian Tracey Weis, who has closely examined the changing dynamics of household labor in post–Civil War Richmond, reiterates this observation. "In the late nineteenth century," Weis writes, "domestic service and housing were both commodities. As such, they served to signify levels of income, refinement, and aspiration."[38]

Domestic Service in Richmond

It is important to note, however, that the hiring of domestic workers was not the sole prerogative of affluent families such as the Dooleys. From 1800 to 1920, the presence of household workers was commonplace in middle-class American homes. Social historians tell us that at any given time during this period, between 15 and 30 percent of all private residences included at least one live-in domestic. The employment of a servant, in fact, became a major perquisite of middle-class status.[39]

In the former slave South, with the region's large population of unemployed and underemployed laborers, lower-middle-class and even some working-class white households could hire help. As women moved into the workforce in shops and factories, they were able to set aside a proportion of their small wages toward assistance with child care, cooking, and cleaning. Some African American households—the most affluent, such as the home of banker Maggie L. Walker, or budding middle-class residences like those Virginia households described by W. E. B. Du Bois in 1898—also retained domestic workers. "Among our well-to-do colored people," Orra Langhorne observed from Lynchburg, Virginia, "it is not uncommon for a servant to be employed."[40]

Richmond, in particular, exceeded the national average for servants per capita in the decades spanning the turn of the century. Census records indicate that Richmond rated second only to Nashville among major American cities in maintaining the highest ratio of domestic workers. An independent 1897 survey determined that Richmond and Washington, D.C., tied for the nation's highest domestic employment rate. For approximately every thirteen people, the study reported, there was one servant.[41]

As in other major cities across the nation, the total number of domestic workers in Richmond declined after 1910. Wage-earning women, who comprised the majority of household employees, sought other opportunities in local factory and shop work or migrated north in search of similar work with better conditions and wages. Many middle-class mistresses became "house-wives," serving the needs of home and family themselves. Articles in ladies magazines and newspaper columns encouraged them to manage the home through new approaches. A 1914 article in the *Richmond Times-Dispatch* (with the long but telling title, "How I Kept House Without a Servant. Number 4 in a Series of Articles on Modern Methods of Business Efficiency Applied to the Household by an Intelligent Woman of Means and Refinement, Who Found It Easier to Do Her Own Work Than to Be Eternally Annoyed by Stupid and Overpaid Servants") actually makes no mention of the vanished help. Instead, it offers such entertainment tips as serving canned tongue, using paper cups, and trying newly developed coffee crystals. After World War I, the widespread availability of electricity, new equipment, efficient plumbing, mass-produced goods, and commercially prepared foods opened up the possibility of maintaining a comfortable lifestyle without the assistance of hired labor.[42]

Large, Specialized Service Staffs

What did distinguish the Dooley household from most others in Richmond—or the United States, for that matter—was the size and makeup of their residential staff. Compared to the typical middle-class residence with its sole "maid-of-all-work," elite homes such as Maymont were set apart by large staffs of male and female employees, each holding a special job title. Emulating aristocratic households in Europe, wealthy Americans embraced this staffing model in the last quarter of the nineteenth century. For them, a home outfitted with bustling, uniformed servants was a requirement for gracious living.[43]

Furthermore, within upper-class households the presence of a male domestic became a significant status symbol. Although Americans continued to retain "hired hands" to help with gardening, animal care, or house maintenance, women made up about 90 percent of household workers by the late nineteenth century. Menservants, as Thorstein Veblen pointed out, almost always required higher wages and therefore were retained only in the most affluent residences. A butler, in particular, became the most valued not only for his skills but for his high visibility—answering doors, greeting callers, and waiting at table. In the North, the acquisition of an English butler became the ultimate fashion coup.[44]

In the South, with its large labor force of African Americans, male domestics were hired with more frequency than in other parts of the country. Men, however, still made up a small percentage of household employees overall. Tracey Weis, identifying a "feminization" of service in Richmond between 1860 and 1890, documents a sharp 80 percent decline in the number of men working as domestic servants. By the time the Dooleys moved into Maymont, less than 10 percent of household employees in the city were male. By 1900, black women made up 95.1 percent of Richmond's domestic employees.[45] Nevertheless, the Dooleys—whether in their Franklin Street home or at Maymont—consistently retained menservants on their employee roster.

Social Ritual

Gilded Age society fostered an adherence to social ceremonies that mandated the presence and participation of domestic servants. Nowhere was this more obvious than in the "front door drama," as Faye Dudden has labeled the elaborate social ritual of calling. This practice of visiting, leaving cards, and receiving visitors became an obligatory activity through which people identified their social circle. The *Richmond Elite Directory* of 1893 devotes a section to calling etiquette "among people of the highest cultivation." The directory's visiting protocol is accompanied by a listing of special messages communicated by the folding of one's calling card—for example, the turning down of the upper left corner denoted "congratulations." Langhorne Gibson Jr. records Richmond's elaborate visitation ritual in the biography of his grandmother, Irene Langhorne Gibson. During calling, he writes, ladies were to avoid the five "d's" in conversation—domestics, domiciles, descendants, disease, and dress.[46]

Butlers and parlor maids served as crucial intermediaries in the screening process for the calling ritual. At Maymont the head butler answered the door, greeted visitors, and showed them in. Collecting their calling cards on a silver tray, he carried them to James or Sallie Dooley, waiting upstairs or behind the closed doors of the library or drawing room.[47] Soon afterwards, the butler returned with the message that Major or Mrs. Dooley was "at home"—that is, receiving the visitor for the requisite twenty-minute visit—or with regrets that he or she was "engaged" or "not at home."[48] The Dooleys depended on a well-trained servant to open doors graciously, to properly address the caller, and—most important—to recognize or assess the visitor's purpose and social standing.

Assessment took place on both sides of the front door. An attendant's appearance or demeanor could shape the visitor's impression of the household—for better or worse. Among Richmond's fashionable residences, many servants were in evidence on calling day and "the butlers really set the tone of the houses," recollected Elizabeth Jeffress, whose grandfather lived near the Dooleys' former residence on Franklin Street. As a girl, Mate Converse took pride in the friendly demeanor of Richard Ruffin, butler to the Melville Branch family: "He knew all my school friends; and they certainly knew him. Richard was fun, not at all severe. And there *were* some butlers in those homes along Franklin, Grace, and Monument, who were quite formidable." In recounting her girlhood years in Richmond, Nancy Langhorne—later the famous Lady Astor, first female member of British Parliament—described the extraprotective butler in her family's West Grace Street household. Allowing no one into the house whom he had not admitted before (including a family friend one memorable day), he would open the door a crack to announce, "Mrs. Langhorne she ain't home!" before shutting it firmly. It was a housemaid, not the butler, who gave Eda Carter Williams and her grandmother an unusual reception in the 1910s. On calling day the two would be driven by carriage to various friends' houses in Richmond. At each stop they would go up the steps and to the door, where a servant would meet them. "Sometimes we would go inside and stay for a little visit," Mrs. Williams remembered; "sometimes we would just leave a card." When they approached one Franklin Street home, they discovered a maid cleaning the stoop. "Her hands were soapy, so she told us: 'Just leave the ticket in my mouth and I'll give it to them.'" More typically, Mrs. Williams clarified with a laugh, a butler would answer the door and offer the card tray.[49]

The Summer Season

During Richmond's oppressive summer heat, upper-class families fled the city for cooler temperatures in the countryside or the mountains. Women and children—with domestic staff in tow—summered in country houses, resorts, and hotels as close as Bon Air, a few miles from the city limits, and as far away as New York. Husbands typically remained behind to attend to business, joining their families on weekends.[50]

Following patterns established by earlier generations of Virginians, Richmonders were particularly attracted to resorts at mineral springs. These had become the locus of a busy summer season; debutantes made their appearances and engagements were announced. Back in Richmond, newspaper society columns followed the arrivals, activities, and departures of the hometown aristocracy with dispatches datelined Warm Springs, Sweet Springs, Hot Springs, and White Sulphur Springs. "The old Dominion had a plethora of sulphur springs where their environs became famous summer resorts," wrote Barbara Trigg Bowen. Recalling her family's habitual summer exodus in the 1880s and '90s, she continued: "From July until late September the city was a bachelor's haven, only the 'bachelors' were married. They settled the families in the Spring of their choice and returned to their offices and to a great deal of Club life until their vacation time came. Later, with increased prosperity a number of Richmonders were buying summer homes in the Blue Ridge Mountain section."[51]

James and Sallie Dooley were among those attracted to the cooler climate of the Blue Ridge. Although no records survive to indicate where they took up summer residence in the late nineteenth century, the couple likely made their way to various popular resorts—including Sweet Springs, where Major Dooley's sister, Florence, resided, having married into the resort's founding family. In 1910 the Dooleys acquired property for a palatial summer residence of their own near Waynesboro, Virginia, in the Blue Ridge Mountains. Named Swannanoa in part, perhaps, for Sallie Dooley's well-known predilection for swans, the marble-encased Italianate abode was ready for them two years later. The mansion—reminiscent of the opulence and scale of the grand summer "cottages" at Newport, Rhode Island—is twice the size of Maymont and includes a Tiffany Studios window depicting Sallie Dooley in her gardens. The 760-acre mountaintop property, maintained year-round by an estate manager and grounds staff, featured terraced flower gardens, vegetable gardens, grape arbors, fruit orchards, and a small working farm with chickens, cows, and hogs.[52]

The new summer mansion also included five servant bedrooms and garage apartments for the chauffeur and head gardener. When relocating from Maymont to Swannanoa for the summer, the Dooleys brought along four to six domestic employees. In June they transported themselves, servants, belongings, and automobiles a hundred miles northwest by railroad. In residence at Swannanoa, they supplemented their staff with temporary local domestics. Relocating a household to the country was a daunting task. The domestic staff "closed" the Richmond house (storing heavy carpets and curtains and draping furnishings with dust sheets) and packed employers' clothing and provisions. In the fall, with the family's return, the staff reversed the long process, unpacking and reopening the city residence.

Meal Preparation and Presentation

The period also brought new expectations for meal preparation and formal presentation—which in turn required additional servant assistance and hours. The dining room became an important space, second only to the drawing room in communicating status and taste. Upper-class mistresses had their tables decorated with a dizzying array of damask cloths, linen napkins, fine china, silver, crystal, and floral centerpieces. A sideboard, serving table, and screen to hide the pantry door became essential dining-room furnishings.[53]

Dining itself became an important social ritual and form of entertainment. Etiquette authorities advocated the hiring of a cook trained in preparing not only standard fare for the household but also French haute cuisine for dinner parties. In looking back on her long career as a cook in private households, one-hundred-year-old Charlotte Jackson noted the changing fashion in the menus of affluent Virginians. She reflected, "In the old days, the food was good and there was plenty of it. It wasn't so much French as it is now." Prescriptive literature further dictated an elaborate presentation style that required more dinnerware, equipment, and knowledgeable servants. Domestics had to master the latest techniques for laying table linens and setting the china, silver, and crystal. During the meal—served *à la Russe* in fashionable households—butlers or waitresses ladled soup, carved meat, and served each course on individual dishes.[54]

Two skilled attendants could serve a multicourse meal with choreographed ease. "Let us suppose a table laid for eight persons, dressed in its best; as attendants, only two persons—a butler and a footman or . . . a neat waiting-maid," writes Mrs. Mary F. Henderson in *Practical Cooking and Dinner Giving* (1887), "and let us suppose some one stationed outside the door in the butler's pantry to do nothing but fetch up, or hand, or carry off dishes one by one." Mrs. Henderson follows with the ideal scenario for service *à la Russe*:

> While guests are being seated, person from outside brings up soup;
> Footman receives soup at door;
> Butler serves it out;
> Footman hands it;
> Both change plates.
> Footman takes out soup, and receives fish at door;
> while butler hands wine;
> Butler serves out fish;
> Footman hands it (plate in one hand, and sauce in the other);
> Both change plates.
> Footman brings in *entrée*, while butler hands wine;
> Butler hands *entrée*;
> Footman hands vegetables;

Both change plates,
Etc., etc.[55]

Before the dessert course, attendants offered finger bowls and "crumbed" the cloth.[56] With a skilled staff managing the meal start-to-finish, the host and hostess could better turn their attention to their guests. Afterwards, employees washed, dried, and polished myriad cooking utensils and dinner-ware, laundered linens, and returned them all to assigned storage spaces.

In the Maymont dining room, the placement of the call button on the fireplace wall, some distance from the table, indicates the Dooleys' reliance on trained employees during mealtimes. The butler, standing at the southern end of the room near the button and pantry door, supervised the arrival and distribution of each course. Sallie Dooley's great-nephew, Fitzhugh Elder Jr. recalls that a second butler attended at the other end of the table. When entertaining on the grandest scale, as at the evening reception and banquet given at Maymont in 1898 for "about four hundred of the most prominent in Richmond's society," the Dooleys hired a professional catering firm from New York for food preparation and service.[57]

No evidence survives that documents the level of supervision Sallie Dooley provided her cook and butlers when it came to meal planning, preparation, or presentation. Oral histories of contemporary Richmond houses indicate that upper-class mistresses participated and supervised in varying degrees. Mate Converse recalled that her mother, Martha Branch, went to the kitchen each morning with a small pad of paper and pencil, sat on one of the chairs, and spoke with the cook about the meals for the day. She, herself, didn't cook, but she did set the menu and "knew if something was done properly." Retired state supreme-court justice Thomas C. Gordon Jr. remembered that his mother also planned the meals, although "she never cooked. [Upper-class] women just didn't in the South." In the Edward Pleasants Valentine household, Mrs. Valentine not only set the menus but also maintained control over daily food supplies. Martha Valentine Cronly remembered: "My mother 'gave out' the provisions each day from the pantry; then they were put on the 'dumb waiter' and pulled by rope to the kitchen which was in the basement." Isabel Scott Anderson, on the other hand, often relied on the discretion and skills of her longtime cook, Hylah Wright, to determine daily menus. Except for special occasions such as dinner parties, which required consultation, "Mrs. Anderson turned it all to me," Mrs. Wright recalled. "She didn't have nothing to do with cooking."[58]

Larger Houses, More Work

The most compelling reason for retaining a large staff was the sheer drudgery of housework, which remained constant and labor intensive. The physical requirements for maintaining opulent residences such as Maymont increased exponentially with size and contents. As houses grew bigger, the number of objects in them multiplied—and so did household chores like picking up, dusting, sweeping, polishing, and washing. Such jobs became more cumbersome as fashion mandated that rooms like those at Maymont be packed with elaborately carved, upholstered furniture, heavy drapes and carpets, and ornate bric-a-brac. "Consumers of these things cannot make way with them in the required manner without help," economist Thorstein Veblen asserted.[59]

While the Dooley estate was situated in the countryside outside Richmond, the Maymont staff still waged daily battle against coal dust. The ubiquitous grit from urban industry and passing trains rode the prevailing breezes. "Coal dust was solid," recalled Maria Bemiss Hoar of her Richmond childhood in the 1910s. "It settled down ... oh goodness, it got things dirty. . . . You kept the windows shut to keep it from getting too bad." In residences with central heat such as the Bemiss home and Maymont, coal dust also entered rooms through the network of furnace ducts. In 1921 James Dooley complained to his business secretary about a partial delivery from Long Coal Company: "Why do they not deliver the balance of the coal? It is very inconvenient to me to have the delivery split, as I have to clean up my house twice, instead of once."[60] More accurately, his domestic employees faced the extra rounds of dusting and sweeping.

Rising Standards of Cleanliness

Scientific findings of the day compounded the burden of housekeeping. The discovery of the tubercle microorganism in 1882 reshaped prescriptive literature. Thereafter, household manuals addressed germ theory and recast housecleaning as an ongoing campaign against disease.[61] In *The Complete Home* (Richmond, 1883), Julia McNair Wright describes invisible "floating particles of disease" in the home. Advocating cleanliness for health's sake, she warns that "spores of small-pox, yellow, typhoid and scarlet fevers, cholera, diphtheria, measles, and kindred diseases are so small that twenty thousand of them, end to end, would not reach the length of an inch; fifty million might be but in a cubic inch." The solution, she argues, comes through strict supervision of servants to ensure thorough cleaning.[62]

It appears that the Dooleys were apprised of current discoveries in bacteriology. Their library at Maymont includes *The Technology of Bacteria Investigation* (1885), a small volume organized by disease types and related research. The design and furnishing of the Maymont's second-floor bathrooms are characteristic of the new sanitation mandates. Ceramic tiles and porcelain, with their nonabsorbent surfaces, could be more easily scrubbed; exposed water and waste pipes were more accessible for cleaning.[63] Sometime after the construction of the house, a small folding sink was retrofitted into the mansion's first-floor coat closet to facilitate hand washing near the water closet.

Stringent standards extended to personal hygiene as well. Middle- and upper-class Americans bathed more frequently than did their forebears. "A daily bath is desirable for both health and cleanliness," Fannie Chase instructs readers in her 1913 etiquette manual, *Good Form and Social Habits*. Bathing each day meant ablutions from a pitcher and washbasin as well as immersion in a bathtub.[64] "Good form," in relation to both hygiene and social expectation, also meant changing clothes more often—sometimes several times a day. "One of the charms of the well-dressed girl lies in her dainty freshness—in her snowy whiteness of her clean shirt-waist, in the spotlessness of her collar and cuffs, her stock, or the ruching that relieves a dark silk waist," Chase asserts.[65] The desire for an increasing number of fresh garments meant more servant hours in the laundry, at the ironing table, and at the employer's wardrobe.

Domestic sanitation reform was not the sole prerogative of women. Mate Converse recalled that her father, Melville Branch, took a particular stand in their Monument Avenue home. Among upper-class households, it had been a longheld custom to assign a personalized napkin ring to each family member. The purpose was to help the individual identify a specific cloth napkin, which was to be used repeatedly for the entire week's meals. "My father thought this was most unhygienic," Mrs. Converse noted. "He insisted that clean napkins be used each time." When the Branch family sat to dinner, there were nine, counting parents, six children, and a grandmother. Of course, she added, the paternal decree had implications for the staff: "My mother estimated that the laundress washed and ironed 125 napkins a week."[66]

Popular literature for middle-class housewives also linked cleanliness with virtue. In a 1902 article, Lavinia Hart urges: "Culture is cleanliness. It is thoroughness. It has to do with clean linen, as well as clean morals. It stands for the lack of smut behind actual doors, no less than behind the inlets and outlets to character."[67]

Personal Service

The quantity *and* quality of clothing worn by the upper classes required their laundresses to attain specific skills in washing, "dry" cleaning (using meal or other absorbent powders and blotting), ironing, and folding. Personal servants were trained in handling special garments, footwear, and hats and in dressing employers appropriately. If care of everyday clothing was labor intensive, formal evening wear warranted extraordinary attention. Mrs. Dooley's personal maid, for instance, would have handled several of her magnificent costumes reserved for grand occasions. These gowns, many documented in newspaper accounts, were mostly European made and fabricated from such costly materials as antique duchesse lace, silk trimmed with white fur, and black velvet. For an 1898 reception at Maymont, "one of the most brilliant events of the season" the *Times-Dispatch* declared, Mrs. Dooley received her guests in a Worth gown of cream brocade, embroidered in silver and pearls.[68]

In his satirical *Theory of the Leisure Class*, Thorstein Veblen considers the importance of apparel in establishing the wearer's social standing. Not only did a gown's costly fabric and trim signify one's ability to pay, but its elaborate cut further signaled her exemption from physical labor. "Therefore," he explains, "pains should be taken in the construction of women's dress, to impress upon the beholder the fact . . . that the wearer does not and can not habitually engage in useful work."[69] In this period lady's maids were summoned day and night to help dress or extricate upper-class mistresses from garments with impossibly complex side and back closings and detachable drapery and trains. While no Maymont employee is identified specifically as "lady's maid" on census or city-directory records, oral histories attest to Sallie Dooley's reliance on domestics for personal service.[70]

Roseann Hester—granddaughter of George and Helen Tatum, a Maymont estate worker and his wife who resided on the property—recalled an occasion when Mrs. Dooley found herself without the assistance of her lady's maid:

> [She] sent a message to my grandmother that she needed some help in getting dressed as her servants, attendants, whatever were not there. Grandma had a baby girl whom she had to get up and get dressed, as well as herself to take to Mrs. Dooley's house. When Grandma got there, she went upstairs and helped her while my grandfather stood at the bottom of the stairs and held the baby (my aunt Helen). When Grandma told me this story, I think we were discussing how much harder it was for my grandmother to go out and help Mrs. Dooley (baby and all) instead of Mrs. Dooley dressing herself. But I'm sure she was so used to having this sort of help that it never crossed her mind to do it any differently.[71]

Valets attended male employers, providing help with bathing, shaving, clothing and shoe care, and dressing. James Dooley, whose wartime injury to the right wrist resulted in a lifelong disability, probably needed some daily assistance with such tasks. Again, no employee is listed in extant records with this particular job title. The butler, however, and/or his assistant, may well have rendered personal service in addition to other household duties. A 1921 letter documents Dooley's preference during a period of sickness for a black male attendant over the services of a white female nurse.[72]

Uniform-ity

The Dooleys had dress standards for their staff as well. Like their wealthy urban counterparts, the couple required household employees to wear livery—that is, special uniforms. According to oral-history accounts, May-mont's housemaids were provided three sets of livery: a gray dress with white apron for day work and cleaning, a black dress with white ruffled apron for afternoon and evenings, and a burgundy dress with white apron detailed with burgundy piping for special occasions. The cook wore a gray uniform, white apron, and white band collar. Relating her childhood impressions of the kitchen staff at Maymont, Audrey Smith recalled several uniformed workers: "One wore a cap. . . . I don't remember her name. But I know she was the boss." The butler and second butler each wore a tailored black or dark gray sack suit and white shirt in the day and a black cutaway coat at night. The Maymont coachman donned a cape and top hat, while the chauffeur wore a military-style jacket (referred to on a clothing-store receipt as an "alp-coat"), leather gauntlets, and a garrison cap.[73]

The imposition of livery on American domestics coincided with growing class distinctions in the last quarter of the nineteenth century. This European custom, prominent in the eighteenth century, fell out of favor in the United States during the Federal period. Like coats of arms and royal titles, livery was associated with aristocratic pretensions. In the 1870s and 1880s, however, wealthy families reintroduced the use of livery in emulation of English practices. Very quickly, a dark dress, white apron, and white cap became the standard apparel required for female servants in middle- and upper-class urban homes. Even maids-of-all-work in modest households were required at least to wear a cap.[74]

Neatly uniformed servants denoted a well-managed household. A 1910 article in the *Ladies Home Journal* pictures various uniforms and aprons. It urges: "Every housekeeper should realize that the appearance of the maids in her house is an indication of her good taste and management, as they, in a measure, set the standard of the establishment from the moment the door is opened." Four years later, a household manual underscored this point, reminding readers: "People are judged, more than they perhaps realize, by the character and appearance of their serving folk."[75]

Liveried servants were customary in the homes of Richmond's high society during the late nineteenth and early twentieth centuries. Oral histories describe a variety of day uniforms for female employees—gray, pink, blue, or striped dress with white apron. The standard dress for evening was consistent among households: a black dress with white or black apron.[76] In his memoirs, James Branch Cabell describes the daily assemblage of uniformed African American nursemaids in Monroe Park: "These ladies wore white caps and large white aprons, befrilled proudly.... None dared to assail [their] authority ... and this was especially true of the parents who paid to each one of them ten dollars a month."[77] Elizabeth Winn, remembering the turn of the century on Franklin Street, recalled that "Mammy" Margaret "wore a white kerchief, and apron."[78] These dress requirements and traditions were maintained into the twentieth century. A 1928 survey conducted by the Richmond Council of Social Agencies noted that of 260 domestic workers interviewed, 214 had been furnished uniforms by employers.[79]

Address, Terminology, and Distinctions of Class and Race

The manner of address and terminology used for household employees reinforced social distance and underscored notions of superiority and subordination between employers and domestic workers. Household manuals, like Emily Holt's *Everyman's Encyclopaedia of Etiquette* (1901), encouraged employers to address servants by first name alone. Holt cautioned, however, against the use of nicknames, as it "encourages that familiarity which, besides being undesirable in itself, renders punctual and exact service impossible."[80] In speaking of domestics in the third person, employers sometimes reverted to "girl" or "boy," no matter the age of the employee.[81]

Abiding by rules of etiquette, Maymont staff members would have addressed their employers as "Major Dooley" and "Mrs. Dooley." In turn, as surviving documents and oral history suggest, the Dooleys and their family members would have addressed household employees by their first names.[82] Jeanette Bailey, daughter of the Maymont head butler, William Dilworth, recalled that "the Dooleys called Papa 'William.'" She also remembered that, in a show of respect for her father, James Dooley told others, "I don't want you calling him by any other name but *Mr. Dilworth*—because that's who he is.... You don't call him by his [first] name."[83]

Oftentimes, southern employers used prefixes for older black domestics such as "Uncle," "Auntie," or "Mammy" in place of "Mister," "Missus," or "Miss." John A. Cutchins, writing of Richmond in the 1880s, recalled:

"['Uncle'] was a courtesy which was due them and also a mark of our affection. Servants, white or colored, are addressed by their names, but children were not permitted to do that; so, although the relationship of master and servant did not then exist, the younger members of the family were taught to call them 'Uncle.' . . . Unfortunately, the *Uncle Tom's Cabin* by Harriet Beecher Stowe in 1851–52 has converted the courteous name 'Uncle' of my boyhood days into an object of ridicule."[84]

Richmonder Mary Tyler McClenahan recalled a particular linguistic differentiation in the early decades of the twentieth century. In the household of her historian father, Douglas Southall Freeman, she was taught to use an *ah* sound when describing a blood-related aunt and a short *a* sound for Auntie, her nursemaid.[85]

Social distance was underscored by the growing use of the title "servant" during the Gilded Age. The word has a rather complicated history in the United States. In the decades between 1790 and 1840, when egalitarian rhetoric prevailed following the Revolutionary War, "servant" fell out of favor in northern states. The term became an anathema because of its general associations with European class systems, colonial indentured servitude, and the adoption of the word in the American South as a euphemism for slaves. In the North, substitutions such as "help" or "domestic" were developed in the 1830s as less-offensive terms for white household employees.[86] In 1858 Michael Byrne in Chicago wrote to his brother-in-law, the senior John Dooley, in Richmond. His letter reveals an awareness of the changing terminology: "Have got no housekeeper yet but have got two servants—I beg their pardon—*helps*—One is an old lady who 'saw better days' & the other a maid of all work—they both work. We send the washing to the city laundry and we use bakers bread, which is equal to another *help*."[87]

The word "servant" nevertheless gained popular currency in American vocabulary after the 1870s.[88] Vassar professor Lucy Salmon conducted an extensive survey of employers and employees at the end of the century. She determined that "servant" came back into use "because of the increase of wealth and consequent luxury in this country, the growing class divisions, and the adoption of many European habits of living and thinking and speaking."[89]

Popular use of the word, alongside the growing requirement of livery, coincided with the expanding number of immigrants entering the American labor force. In the second half of the nineteenth century, successive waves of immigration brought hundreds of thousands of laboring poor from Ireland, Germany, Scandinavia, and Eastern Europe. The northeastern United States bore the brunt of the massive influx, and by the 1870s immigrant household workers in that region far outnumbered native-born whites, who preferred factory jobs to the stigma of service. The dominance of service by immigrants spurred lively commentary in newspapers, periodicals, and household manuals. Employers rather quickly became disillusioned with and even hostile toward the "strangers in the gates" who had become such an important part of their households.[90]

Ethnic, religious, and racial differences fanned tensions and widened the social gap between employers and employees. Professor Salmon observed that with the predominance of "the foreign-born and negro element," a more stringent "class line" developed within middle- and upper-class households.[91] The concepts of respecting one's "betters" and of "knowing one's place" entered public discourse at the time. In her household manual, Emily Holt contends that "neither servant nor mistress profits by any lowering of the proper barriers set between them; and it is false consideration as well as unmeaning to use the term *hired help.* . . . No self-respecting man or woman resents the use of the word servant, or its meaning." Reinforced by social Darwinism and pseudoscientific race theories, the notion of class privilege was closely identified with white Anglo-Saxon America. Present-day historian Alan Trachtenberg argues that during the Gilded Age "social contrasts reached a pitch without precedent in American life outside the slave South."[92]

Below the Mason-Dixon Line, where racial divisions and domestic work were inextricably linked, the term "servant" had been applied consistently over time to black household workers, both slave and free. As one British observer commented in the 1850s, "the negro is not a help; he is emphatically a servant." Richmonder Gordon McCabe noted that household laborers in the antebellum South were "servants" and "never called 'slaves' by gentle-folk." The term persisted after emancipation and into the twentieth century. In 1901, Virginian Orra Langhorne maintained: "When a Southerner speaks of servants, negroes are always understood. Irish Biddy,

English Mary Ann, German Gretchen, and Scandinavian maids are as yet unknown factors. . . . Black Dinah holds the fort."[93]

That southerners—and more specifically Richmonders—might habitually equate the word "servant" with black household workers was tested in an unusual court case at the beginning of the new century. When Lewis Ginter, whose cigarette empire made him one of the wealthiest men in Virginia, crafted a final codicil to his will, he expressed a desire that his estate pay "to all servants in my employ at the time of my death, $50 each." Following the multimillionaire's death in 1897, not only did his domestic employees come forward, but so did an additional one hundred laborers from his country estate. After six years of legal maneuvers and appeals, *Ginter's Executors v. Shelton et al.* was decided in the commonwealth's Supreme Court of Appeals in 1903. Upholding a more generic meaning of the term and disregarding preconceived notions of job description or race, the appellate court upheld the decision that the estate must distribute the specified bequest to various farmhands, blacksmiths, quarrymen, and engineers once employed by Lewis Ginter.[94]

In keeping with regional tradition and fashion, James and Sallie Dooley used the term "servant" when referring to household laborers—whether in childhood, when slaves tended them, or as adults, with a contingency of waged employees. In his Civil War diary, James Dooley's brother John describes the slave Ned Haines as "our black servant boy." A lifetime later in the 1920s, Major Dooley sent written instructions arranging for an automobile to pick up and transport his "four negro servants."[95]

The "Servant Problem"

Whatever Americans called their household workers, "good help" was viewed as an increasingly rare commodity in the Gilded Age. The topic of domestic workers, as Langhorne Gibson notes, was considered taboo in polite conversation among ladies. Nevertheless, few subjects commanded as much attention in women's literature as the perceived decline in the quantity and quality of household laborers. In articulating the "Servant Problem"— whether between friends or in the popular press—employers were dissatisfied with the availability, competency, and high turnover rate of workers.[96]

Training a new staff member was a "serious piece of business" according to Harriet Spofford, who found unskilled workers the most frustrating aspect of the "Servant Problem." Mistresses, she noted, had to endure the incompetent employee who "shatters the delicate edges of every piece of your best china set with rough handling, cracks your engraved glass, and melts the hafts off your knives with too hot water, scorches her sign manual on your table-cloths with too hot irons, burns your dinner to a crisp with neglect." After months of instruction, during which the employer has trained the worker in proper procedure and the routine of the house, she must then "receive notice of intended departure, and have it all to do over again with the next one."[97]

Being mistress of a large household with a specialized staff required organizational skills, patience, and diplomacy. In the summer of 1903, one prominent Richmond mistress wrote her mother of a bleak episode with a disgruntled maid: "Pride always comes before the fall. When I was boasting to you a short while ago of my great domestic comfort I might have known it was too good to last. We have had the most horrible row. Little Bettie is the only servant speaking to all the others, and tonight Ocie is sitting in the middle of the floor crying and packing her trunk to leave tomorrow morning early. . . . I have been having as rough a time as I like. . . . and I'm afraid I don't like my responsibilities either."[98]

According to *McClure's Magazine* in 1910, employers had two primary criteria for a good employee: "The first quality sought in a servant is loyalty; the second is servility." The article further describes the fierce battle ensuing in homes across the United States: "On the one side are ranged a million housewives, fighting for the ordered comfort of home. On the other side is a ragged army of conscripts, working joylessly, struggling hopelessly, deserting whenever possible, shirking when desertion is impossible. Naturally, mistress blames maid; and, also naturally, maid blames mistress."[99] Household manuals included suggestions for managing the "help," at times pointing out the shortcomings of both employee and employer. Offering a "Summing up of the Servant Problem," Ethel Cushing urged: "Servants must be trained to the knowledge of their various duties and a firm discipline maintained. On the other hand, employers may add much to the loyalty given by servants if they pay them promptly, make them comfortable, and treat them as human beings."[100]

The fact that the great majority of American domestics were either immigrants or African Americans helped widen the gap between employers and employees. In *The Servant Girl Question* (1881), Harriet Spofford yearns for "our own people . . . servants of our own race, religion, and habits." Otherwise, she warns, "interests are so utterly apart, union is hardly possible, there is always something foreign in the household, and there is disintegration at the very foundation of home."[101]

In literature of the period, African American domestics were deemed less difficult than were immigrant servants and, through their long association with slavery, inherently more submissive. One household manual praises the "old-type Southern negro, who is a product of our own land. This class is passing into the new fields of enterprise open to all. But if managed with a gentle firmness that we use with children, these servants rose to heights of efficiency and loyalty that could not be surpassed."[102] In the South, however, a distinction was being drawn between a new generation of black workers and their enslaved forebears. "Every person who was old enough to know anything at the close of the war," contends a 1900 editorial in the *Richmond Times*, "knows that the negroes, especially what was known as the 'house negro,' that is those who had been in close contact with the whites, were far superior, in the matter of manners and morals at least, to the negroes as a class of to-day. They were genteel and they had some individuality and character. Take an old time Virginia carriage driver or butler of to-day and you will find a man of sense, a man of character and in many respects a polished gentleman."[103]

Southern Service in Black and White

James and Sallie Dooley learned from childhood on to expect care, comfort, and service from African American attendants—whether enslaved or waged. As adults, the couple showed a consistent preference for black employees that was in keeping with hiring patterns of middle- and upper-class households in Richmond and across the South. In 1900, for example, nine out of ten domestics in all southern cities were African American women.[104] Nearly four decades later, authors of a WPA study in Virginia noted: "The traditional excellence of the Negro cook and nurse-maid and the low wages for which they can be employed create a steady demand."[105]

White domestics were not unheard of in affluent Richmond residences. During an extended trip to England in 1912, Frederic and Elise Scott hired Percy Thornton and brought him back to Richmond as their chauffeur. Former Dooley neighbor T. C. Williams Jr. hired an Irish housekeeper in his West Franklin Street home. The Monument Avenue household of John Kerr Branch and his New York–born wife, Beulah Gould, included a French woman named Jeanne. This lady's maid assisted Mrs. Branch with dressing and bathing, but she also made many of her employer's clothes, having taken courses at the Parisian dressmaking firm of Worth. The 1920 census indicates that among the residence's nine servants were an Irish butler, two Irish housemaids, a Norwegian cook, a Swedish second butler, and a Swedish maid. The Branch's chauffeur was a white man from New York.[106]

Making arrangements through New York agencies, the most affluent Richmond households could also acquire a French governess. Mate Converse noted that these young women were typically unmarried—and that there was generally a high turnover in staffing. "Their primary task was to teach children manners and to speak French," Mrs. Converse continued. "They were never referred to as 'servants' and always took their meals with the family, except during dinner parties." She recalled in particular a Mademoiselle Mouton, who would dress up her brothers Read and Pat for excursions. To keep them in line, the governess would threaten to kiss the little boys in public. "That way, they behaved," Mrs. Converse stated. "She had complete control."[107]

Although a series of black coachmen and chauffeurs served the Dooleys throughout the decades spanning the turn of the twentieth century, they also hired white chauffeur-mechanics—brothers James and C. Hamilton Fitzgerald from Nelson County—in the 1910s–1920s. During her childhood visits to Maymont, Audrey Smith was intrigued with the horses and carriages. In remembering the uniformed coachmen, she noted: "The first one I saw was a white man. He had a top hat and a cape around his shoulders. I don't know their names, because you weren't allowed to talk to them."[108]

In a review of the Dooleys' known employment history for the household staff, the hiring of a white immigrant (German-born Emily Lack-

miok) stands out as an anomaly. The absence at Maymont of Irish domestics—ubiquitous in the North—may seem unusual considering James
Dooley's own ethnic heritage. His deep concern over the plight of famine
victims in Ireland might have extended to finding work for Irish Catholic
refugees in America.[109] The Virginia-born Dooleys, however, likely found
themselves more comfortable with African American workers in their
home than with immigrants unassimilated to American ways. The couple
would have more closely shared aspects of southern culture—language,
foodways, tradition—with their black staff.[110] In recalling her childhood
at Mirador in Albemarle County, Nancy Lancaster described a "strong
understanding" between white families and their black servants in Virginia: "You feel something with them you don't feel about foreign servants
that have come from a different part of the world. . . . We shared a common heritage, a common past. They had known the old ways, knew the
way things were done, as much as we did."[111]

With the "old ways" of the South came patterns of paternalism on one
side and deference on the other, the white-black relationship formed during the antebellum slave regime. When the Dooleys created the opulent
world of Maymont, emancipation had freed African Americans thirty
years earlier. Nevertheless, an entrenched racial code remained firmly in
place. Concerning "what Southern white people deem the 'natural relations,'" Orra Langhorne wrote in 1884, "[it] had been taught by pulpit,
press, and public speakers, in hall and cot, everywhere and at all times, that
whenever the two races come into contact, the white man must rule, and
the black man must serve." In his later assessment of the era, historian C.
Vann Woodward noted that "southern conservatives believed that every
properly regulated society had superiors and subordinates, that each class
should acknowledge its responsibilities and obligations."[112]

The old relations, however, began to change. Charles W. Chesnutt,
the best-known black novelist in the early twentieth century, articulated
the southern version of the "Servant Problem" in his book, *The Marrow of
Tradition* (1901). A leading character in the story, Major Carteret, complains
to a longtime family servant, Mammy Jane: "The old times have vanished,
the old ties have ruptured. The old relations of dependence and loyal obe-
dience on the part of the colored people, the responsibility of protection

and kindness upon that of whites, have passed forever. The young negroes are too self-assertive. . . . They are not content with their station in life."[113]

In 1890 Orra Langhorne noted an assertiveness and restlessness among the new generation of black domestics as well. Observing the response of their employers, she wrote, "The ex-slaveholders . . . feel the discomfort of rude and irregular service more than any other people on the earth would do, because under the former dispensation, to which the white 'Southron' will always look back as 'the good old times,' such things as changing servants, except in case of death or pecuniary disaster, were almost unknown."[114] In an attempt to diagnose the economic challenges of Virginia and the South in 1889, Lewis H. Blair encouraged the "elevation of the Negro." Blair described white paternalism as fleeting and circumstantial: "Most of our kindness to the negroes proceeds from the standpoint of condescension, and of assumed caste superiority, and we expect it to be received with humility and from a feeling of acknowledged caste inferiority; and if not so received by the negroes, they are thought impudent . . . and the fountain of our kindness soon dries up."[115]

In the decades following emancipation, African Americans strove to exercise new political, geographical, and economic freedoms. White southerners, however, tended to hold tightly to prewar expectations, traditions, and a continuing observance of color caste. A new century did not erase old expectations. In 1905 Oswald Garrison Villard observed: "In the South—and here is where the rub comes—there is a positive belief and a sharp insistence that the servant class is destined to servitude for all time; that it is inferior by reason of skin-color . . . and that it ought not to assume any other manners or expect any other treatment." With economic power firmly on the side of the employer, the established social structure—dominance of whites and subordination of blacks—remained intact in the working relationship of the private household.[116]

The Age of Jim Crow

The Maymont era—roughly 1890 to 1925—coincides exactly with the Age of Jim Crow, described by historian Leon Litwack as the most violent and repressive period in the history of race relations in the United States. The term "Jim Crow" was taken from a minstrel-show character developed in the North before the Civil War. In the late nineteenth century, the name came to signify the subordination and separation of black people by white people through law, custom, and coercion.[117]

As African Americans began to exercise new freedoms and to test the tenets of white supremacy, a backlash developed that nullified their participation in the democratic process. In 1883 the U.S. Supreme Court declared the Civil Rights Act of 1875 unconstitutional, stripping black Americans of equal rights to public accommodations and jury participation. The restrictive climate led to the high court's 1896 upholding of the *Plessy v. Ferguson* decision, which established the doctrine of "separate but equal" in American life and law.[118] Racial segregation, enforced socially in the North, was translated into state law in the South. W. E. B. Du Bois, describing the era's reversals, wrote: "The slave went free; stood a brief moment in the sun; then moved back again toward slavery."[119]

While a racial divide had remained fairly intact in Virginia following Reconstruction, the commonwealth's government played an active role in codifying it in the early twentieth century. Between 1900 and 1925, the General Assembly enacted a series of laws that obstructed the black vote and mandated segregation in schools, railroads, hospitals, churches, cemeteries, public transportation, and assembly. In streetcars, state regulations required the separation of passengers by race—whites to be seated in the front, blacks in the back. Despite organized protests and boycotts by the African American community between 1904 and 1907, the color line in streetcars remained intact and was incorporated into the bus system that followed. The city of Richmond, supported and applauded by editorials from leading white newspapers, enforced Jim Crow laws requiring such separation of black and white citizens. The *Richmond Times* urged in 1900 that segregation be "applied in every relation of Southern life" on the grounds that "God Almighty drew the color line and it cannot be obliterated. The negro must stay on his side of the line and the white man must stay on his side, and the sooner both races recognize this fact and accept it, the better it will be for both."[120]

Some employers interceded on behalf of their African American employees through such actions as acquiring goods for them from whites-only stores or sending automobiles to transport them to and from work. Nevertheless, white Richmonders generally accepted segregation laws and practices. Maria Hoar recalled that, as a child in the 1910s and 1920s, she was aware of the "separate-but-equal" laws. "It just was what was.... It's like saying the light's on or the light's off," she noted. "You never thought about it being fair or unfair. It was just what existed. Then we began to be conscious that it wasn't what it ought to be. You began to feel aggressive about it, that it should be changed; it ought to be changed. It took a while."[121]

Unfortunately, the broad movement against African Americans in this period did not stop at the political level. The fears and prejudices that fostered Jim Crow restrictions were also manifested in violence. In the South, lynching became rampant; between 1890 and 1917, three thousand black men and women were tortured and murdered by mobs—an average of two to three people a week. Of these, 19 percent were lynched following accusations of rape—sometimes on such thin evidence as a suspect glance. Public perception and outrage, fueled by a growing number of pamphlets, articles, and books calling for the defense of white womanhood, served to elevate sexual assault to the generally perceived cause for lynching. Mob rule also sought revenge for such offenses as blacks' attempting to participate in labor-union activities, registering to vote, bringing suit, or simply being disrespectful to whites. Racial tensions escalated in Danville, Virginia, when a white store clerk stumbled over the foot of one of two black men walking in the other direction. The subsequent Danville Riot of 1883 resulted in the shooting deaths of one white and four black men—including a black policeman. In some regions, the vigilante Ku Klux Klan enforced racial separation. Reorganized and strengthened in 1910, the white supremacist movement saw its membership reach its highest numbers in the 1920s. Both Klan activity and incidents of lynching were significantly lower in Virginia than in other southern states. In fact the Klan was widely denounced in Richmond's white and black newspapers alike when it paraded and held a rally in the City Auditorium in 1922. Nevertheless, as historian Edward Ayers emphasizes, for African Americans "the New South was a notoriously violent place."[122]

As antiblack sentiment reached a zenith in all geographical regions of white America, popular culture also played a role in shoring up the color line. Best-selling novels such as Thomas Nelson Page's *Red Rock* (1898) and Thomas Dixon's *The Leopard's Spots* (1902) fanned white fear of black violence. In 1915 the new film medium celebrated Ku Klux Klan reprisals against African Americans in D. W. Griffith's epic film *Birth of a Nation*, adapted from Dixon's novel *The Clansman* (1905).[123] At the same time, popular arts romanticized the paternalism of the antebellum slave system with what African American philosopher Alain Locke described as a "cotton-patch and cabin-quarters formula." The "old plantation Negro" became a regular feature in books, articles, and poems, one of the earliest examples being Thomas Nelson Page's anthology, *In Ole Virginia* (1887). The stereotype flourished as well in contemporary paintings, illustrations, songs, advertisements, and commodity packaging.[124] Uncle Tom, Auntie, Dinah, and Mammy caricatures abounded, perpetuating the notion that African Americans as a whole were childlike, dependent, and in need of white benevolence and supervision.[125]

For whites concerned about the advances of the "New Negro" who would not stay in his or her "place," the meek and servile stereotype was a reassuring and effective foil. In his 1904 book, *The Negro: The Southerner's Problem*, Thomas Nelson Page parades a series of happy "old-time" servants—mammies, butlers, and maids—that, he assures the reader, once graced the antebellum household in the South. By contrast, he continues, young "Negroes" of the present day had turned insolent, even vicious. The novelist predicts, however, that "the great Anglo-Saxon race, which is dominant, and the Negro race, which is amiable, if not subservient, will adjust their differences more in accordance with the laws . . . and the old feeling of kindliness, which seems, under the stress of antagonism, to be dying away, will once more reassert itself." In the same year, Page's supremacist views struck a more militant chord in an article for the *North American Review*. The Virginian directly linked the nation's increased number of lynchings with the granting of civil rights to blacks. As a result, he contended, the "New Issue" acted out its notions of equality through acts of assault and rape.[126]

A few months later, Mary Church Terrell, charter member and first president of the National Association of Colored Women, responded in the same magazine:

Strange as it may appear, illiterate negroes . . . are coddled and caressed by the South. To the educated cultivated members of the [white] race, they are held up as bright and shining examples of what a really good negro should be. The dictionary is searched in vain . . . for the dear old "mammy" or faithful old "uncle," who can neither read nor write, and who assure their white friends they would not, if they could.

On the other hand, no language is sufficiently caustic, bitter and severe, to express the disgust, hatred and scorn which Southern gentlemen feel for what is called the "New Issue," which being interpreted, means negroes who aspire to knowledge and culture, and who have acquired a taste for the highest and best things in life. At the door of the "New Issue," the sins and shortcomings of the whole race are laid.[127]

The Dooleys, Richmond's African American Community, and the Maymont Staff

Little remains to guide our understanding of James and Sallie Dooley's interaction with the African American workers in their home or with Richmond's black community at large during these tumultuous decades. By examining surviving documents within the broader context of the era's political and social landscape, we gain some general impressions of their perceptions and concerns.

James Dooley entered Virginia politics in the tempestuous years just after the Civil War. Under the terms of the 1867 Reconstruction Act, the federal government nullified the commonwealth's government and reorganized the state as Military District Number One. Virginia—like all former Confederate states—remained under military control and the occupation of thousands of Union soldiers until it crafted a state constitution that upheld universal male suffrage and the Fourteenth Amendment, which granted citizenship to African Americans. A constitutional convention convened in 1867, led by abolitionist John C. Underwood and comprised of a delegation of former Whigs and both white and black Radical Republicans. After two years of heated debate and compromise, a new constitution emerged with the required components that allowed Virginia's readmittance to the Union in 1870.[128]

Twenty-seven-year-old James Dooley was among those who spoke out against the participants and processes of the constitutional convention. In 1868 he was appointed secretary to a political association made up of "citizens of Richmond of Irish birth and descent." In a speech quoted in the *Richmond Daily Dispatch*, Dooley railed against the convention's "miserable production of twenty-four negroes, scarcely able to read their own printed work, fourteen renegade Virginians, fit associates for them, and twenty-seven scallawags [*sic*], carpet-baggers, and miserable political adventurers from the North." The article printed the group's eight-point resolution, which begins with the pledge that the assembled would work "to vindicate their respect for the organic law, and their fealty to their own color." Within three years, James Dooley found a political home with the newly formed Conservative (Democratic) Party—an alliance of old state Whigs, Democrats, and even a number of black moderates—who banded together to unseat the Radical Republicans. In 1871 the Conservatives gained control of both branches of state government, counting among their ranks Dooley, who began the first of three consecutive terms in the House of Delegates.[129]

Serving in the General Assembly between 1871 and 1877, Delegate Dooley worked alongside Virginia's first African American legislators. The official record for his first session documents his willingness to allow a small breach in the traditional racial divide. Dooley "voted yea to having ministers of several churches in the city, regardless of color, to be alternately invited to open the house with prayer." At the same time, the number of black delegates and senators had begun to dwindle as a result of Conservative Party policies. Beginning in 1871, the legislature redrew the boundaries of congressional districts to break up black majorities. The gerrymandering resulted in the formation of Richmond's famous "Wall Street of black America," Jackson Ward, but it also diminished black office holding across the state by a third.[130]

More detrimental, however, to the participation of black Virginians in the political process was the Conservative Party's institution of a poll tax. In a complicated series of maneuvers, the legislature passed a funding bill in 1871 to pay down the commonwealth's massive prewar debt. The "Funders," with whom James Dooley identified, believed that this previous obligation took precedent over other financial needs, present and future. The commitment to pay off the debt, made difficult by a nationwide financial panic in 1873, resulted in budget shortfalls and severe cuts in state services—particularly devastating to Virginia's nascent public-school system. The Conservatives responded in 1875 by making the payment of the capitation tax—a preexisting "headcount" tariff that had heretofore produced limited revenue—a new prerequisite to voting. A month after a public referendum instituted the poll tax as a constitutional amendment, James Dooley introduced a bill "to enforce the amendments to the constitution concerning the capitation tax and the right of suffrage." It was passed by both House and Senate in March 1877. The requirement effectively shut out many poor and working-class men—both black and white—from the polls.[131]

By the end of Dooley's third term in 1877, the commonwealth was ensnared in a full-blown budget crisis. Despite an open letter urging him to run for reelection—signed by more than one hundred members of the Conservative Party and published in the *Daily Dispatch*—James Dooley retired from public office to tend to the "condition and pressure of my business."[132] He left just as a disgruntled faction of the Conservative Party was mounting a campaign for the "readjustment," or repudiation of the prewar debt. The resulting Readjuster Party—led by William Mahone—formed an interracial coalition with the Republican Party to gain control of state government from 1879 to 1883. During these years the Readjusters promoted African American advancements in office holding, suffrage, jury service, and civic appointments. They also repealed the poll tax in 1882.[133]

Former Conservative "Funders" were, for the most part, absorbed by the Democratic National Party during the 1880 presidential campaign. In the early 1880s Virginia's Democrats made headway against the Readjusters by waging a white-solidarity campaign. White voters were warned that by supporting the Readjusters and "Negro rule," they would undermine political and social racial hierarchy. Invigorated further by Democrat Grover Cleveland's presidential victory in 1885, the party gained enough momentum to secure control over state government for decades to come. Between 1890 and 1925 a Democratic majority would propose and implement a series of Jim Crow laws, mandating the separation of races in the commonwealth. And, in order to correct the "mistakes" of the 1868 Underwood Convention and Readjuster reform that followed, Democratic delegates convened in 1901 to write a new state constitution.[134]

James Dooley's career as an elected official ended in 1877, but his interest and influence in Virginia politics continued through the late nineteenth and into the early twentieth centuries. He left no record of his personal views on race. However, whether as an Irish Conservative, Conservative Democrat, or "life-long Democrat" (as he described himself in an open letter to President Cleveland published in 1893), he aligned himself with political parties that generally opposed black political advancement. On June 26, 1902, Dooley was invited to serve as one of ten prestigious toastmasters at a banquet, headed up by Governor Andrew Jackson Montague, that celebrated the drafting of a revised Virginia constitution. Representing Richmond, Dooley congratulated convention delegates for rescuing Virginia from the peril of "cupidity, ignorance and barbarism" and hailed the advent of "an honest and enlightened suffrage."[135] The primary challenge of the previous, yearlong constitutional convention was to bring about African American disfranchisement without legally violating the Fourteenth and Fifteenth Amendments to the U.S. Constitution. This was accomplished through new voter criteria that included not only a poll tax—this time paid six months in advance—but the ability of the voter, on demand of the polling official, to read and explain any section of the state constitution. It proved effective. Whereas Richmond had 6,000 registered black voters in 1900, in three years the number dropped to 760; during the same period, Jackson Ward alone saw a dramatic decline from 3000 to 33.[136]

In the year before he died, James Dooley continued to hold allegiance to the Democratic Party. In 1921 the state Republican Party declared itself a "white man's party" to entice independent or Democratic votes. In a letter to his business secretary, Dooley noted that "I voted at the [Democratic] primary election . . . and do not feel that there is any sufficient reason, in a Virginia state election for going with the negro party."[137]

As his active political career diminished and his fortunes grew, James Dooley shifted his focus to philanthropy. In the early twentieth century, he and Mrs. Dooley contributed large sums during their lifetimes and also left bequests to such causes as Saint Joseph's Orphan Asylum, the establishment of a municipal library, and the construction of a hospital for children. Upholding the segregationist system of the times, these institutions served the white community only. Surviving business correspondence, however, offers some record of James Dooley's awareness and contributions to African American causes as well. In the early 1920s, he contributed to the Afro-American Old Folks' Home in Jackson Ward. At the same time, Dooley sent funds to help pay the school fees of Virginia Union College student Thomas L. Dabney. The young man, a World War I veteran, kept him apprised of his progress by mail.[138] An advocate of educational advancement and reform, James Dooley wrote a letter to the *Times-Dispatch* urging that a mandatory school-attendance law in Virginia be enforced. Pointing out that only 35 percent of white children were regular attendants, he closed his letter suggesting that black families already held a high regard for education: "The parents of the negro children, however poor they may be, need no compulsory enactment on this subject."[139]

In the age of Jim Crow, even James Dooley's prestige and wealth could not fully protect Maymont's African American employees from the sting of segregationist practices. Writing from Swannanoa in 1921, he asked that two automobiles be hired to pick up his family and staff from the Richmond train station. The following day, he wrote his business secretary again to clarify: "Tell Taliaferro, in engaging the taxis, to be sure to have it understood that one of them is for four negro servants. Last year, the chauffeur refused to take the servants and made us pay for the cab, because, when engaged, it was not stated that they were negroes."[140] Indeed, business receipts from 1920 include an invoice for five dollars from the Richmond Taxicab Company for two automobiles. At bottom, secretary W. C. Bentley noted: "325 [invoice item number] was for hauling servants to house. Other car with white driver refused to haul colored."[141]

Louis Taliaferro, Maymont's white estate manager, may have been recalling attempts by James Dooley to protect his employees when he was interviewed a decade later by the *Richmond Times-Dispatch*. "Major Dooley had the most even disposition," he was quoted as saying, "... never allowing anyone to know when or if he was worried and this quality was transferred to the servants who revered him." Sallie Dooley, who supervised the estate manager and his crew in the ornamental plantings around the estate, received a less enthusiastic endorsement as an employer. "Mrs. Dooley is also held in fond remembrance by Taliaferro," the 1933 article relates. "Although she was commonly considered irritable and nervous at times, Taliaferro says that he understood how to deal with her and never crossed her."[142]

Oral history offers a softer image. In listening to stories of Maymont from her grandmother Hannah Walker Kenney and other Walker siblings who were former Maymont employees, Frances Jones commented, "I didn't get the sense from them that Mrs. Dooley was a very hard task-mistress."[143] Audrey Smith noted that her mother, Maymont lady's maid Georgia Anderson, maintained genial feelings for the Dooleys: "I never heard my Mama or Miss Fannie [Waddy] or anyone say anything disparaging about either one," she recalled. While conceding that Louis Taliaferro's assessment of Sallie Dooley as "nervous" had some merit, she continued: "She was like any other woman that had been pampered and spoiled by her husband, and who was not too familiar with everyday activities—what it cost, what it entailed. . . . Not being in the world where you had to work for everything . . . it's no problem to do this and do that. They've designated somebody to take care of that fully. And if they didn't measure up, they could hire someone else."[144]

In her will, probated after 1925, Sallie Dooley provided substantial bequests to eight staff members as a final gesture of care and appreciation. The remembrance of domestic employees in wills was a common practice among the upper-class families in Richmond. An assessment of probate records from thirty contemporary elite households, however, reveals that her gifts generally exceeded the average bequest amount.[145] Louis Taliaferro, whose lifetime tenure at Maymont was assured in James Dooley's will three years earlier, was granted two thousand dollars. Mrs. Dooley also bequeathed one thousand dollars each to her chauffeur, butler, cook, lady's maid, and general maid. The second butler received five hundred dollars and the kitchen maid one hundred dollars. While these gifts pale in comparison to the millions the couple left to charity and public concerns, the amounts are generous next to the staff's monthly wages, which ranged between twenty dollars and one hundred dollars per month. One of Maymont's domestic employees returned to Maymont after Sallie

Dooley's death as a guide and maid at the newly established Dooley Museum. Her foster daughter recalls that Georgia Anderson—while not remembered with a bequest—was employed by the city of Richmond on the earlier recommendation of Mrs. Dooley.[146]

Bonds of Affection

These fragments from oral histories and other documents offer some suggestion of the Dooleys' regard for members of their household staff. Past and present testimonies from contemporary households demonstrate that families could form deep attachments for domestic employees. In her recollections of her four years in the Executive Mansion when her husband served as Virginia's governor, Etta Donnan Mann produced a five-page tribute to butler Winston Edmunds. Her husband, William Hodges Mann, has the final word in the chapter, declaring Edmunds "a real old Virginia gentleman" who was respected by the prominent and distinguished men of the commonwealth. Mary Wingfield Scott, recalling her grandparents' household on West Franklin Street in the 1880s and 1890s, wrote at length about the men and women who worked there: Rice, the unflappable butler; Louis, the "black angel on the coach box"; and Rose, the maid who served for fifty years. Thomas, a younger butler who resided with his wife in rooms over the stables, was deemed "a very intelligent man, sweet and kind."[147] Speaking of the long hours and duties of domestic employees in her parents' home in the 1910s, Maria Hoar observed, "They worked hard . . . they didn't sit and twiddle their thumbs." Moreover, she affirmed, "they had much more talent, much more ability than most of us."[148]

The bond that formed between children and nursemaids could be especially strong and lasting. Because the Dooleys were childless, they had no need for a nursemaid on the staff roster at Maymont. Nevertheless, child-care providers figured prominently among domestic workers during the Gilded Age. In Richmond white families turned to the black community for midwives, baby nurses (assisting the first few months after childbirth), and nursemaids. "The mammies had creative ways of keeping the children in order," noted Mate Converse. She recalled that when she was a child a small angel figurine sat on the mantle in her bedroom. Naming it Tinkerbell, she and her nursemaid, Maggie Berry Brown, often admired it together. "Well, when I was naughty, it would vanish entirely!" she continued. "Nothing was said, it was just gone. . . . It would come back when I became good enough." When Mate Converse needed assistance with her own infants during the 1930s and 1940s, she sent for Maggie Brown to bring her creative skills to her household in Roanoke and New York City.[149]

John Cutchins, looking back to his childhood in Richmond in the 1880s, firmly states in his memoirs that "the two people who had more to do with my bringing up and my being here today were my mother and my mammy. I am forever grateful to both for their love, their care, and their teachings."[150] Cleiland Donnan, who taught dance and etiquette in Richmond for four decades, recalled the love and devotion of the African American woman who labored in her childhood home. In fact, she credits Susie Byrd for saving her life. "When I got scarlet fever, it was highly contagious," Mrs. Donnan noted. "People were dying of it all around, yet Susie did not run away. The neighbors would come as far as the gate— maybe leave a little custard. But she was right there."[151]

We have found no such warm remembrances of household workers by James and Sallie Dooley. Sallie Dooley, however—looking back sixty years to her own childhood—composed a dedication for *Dem Good Ole Times* that reads: "In Memory of the Dear Old Southern Mammies Whose Love and Fidelity Were the Inspiration of this Book."[152]

Dem Good Ole Times

The single primary document that offers glimpses of Sallie Dooley's perceptions of African Americans is her novel, *Dem Good Ole Times*, published in 1906. Capitalizing on the current popularity of dialect literature by such writers as Joel Chandler Harris, Paul Laurence Dunbar, and Virginia-born Thomas Nelson Page, Mrs. Dooley created the reminiscences of old Ben, "Mistiss' faithful Hade Gardner, in dem good ole times befo de war."[153] Drawing from experiences in her girlhood home and at Locust Grove, with its large slave community, Sallie Dooley offers readers reassurances that harmony once prevailed under a racially hierarchical society. Black people, her novel contends, are happiest when owned and managed by wise and giving white folks. In return, white owners are blessed with good and faithful service.[154]

For her first and only publication, Sallie Dooley did not have to look far for literary models for her story of "local color." Among the extant Dooley books in the Maymont House library are several novels by Thomas Nelson Page, including an 1888 edition of *In Ole Virginia, or Mars Chan and Other Stories*. The Dooleys also owned the 1903 edition of Thomas Dixon's *The Leopard's Spots*, produced by Doubleday, Page and Company—the same New York house that would publish *Dem Good Ole Times* three years later. Learning from these and other authors, Sallie Dooley crafted a tale of Old South sentimentality punctuated with New South anxiety about race and class.

In reading *Dem Good Ole Times*, we might surmise that Mrs. Dooley perceived aspects of the story as factual and her narration as a loving homage to the slave servants of her childhood. At the same time, the romantic racialism of *Dem Good Ole Times* is in keeping with a widespread apologist trend in the late nineteenth century that defended and idealized the former slave system.[155] As complaints about the "Servant Problem" and the "Negro Question" heated up in popular literature, the model domestic—efficient, faithful, deferential, and willing to serve—was identified as the old plantation slave. The year before Sallie Dooley's book was published, Oswald Garrison Villard told the National Negro Business League: "The old household servant of slavery days . . . is now almost deified. He is not only celebrated in song and story, but he is used to justify the whole institution of slavery. To hear people talk in Georgia or Virginia we might easily think that every slave was a Chesterfieldian butler or a mistress in the art of old-time Virginia cooking."[156]

The picture Mrs. Dooley offers through Ben's memories of the Old South is familial, paternalistic, and generally rosy. Contemporary reviews in Richmond newspapers note a dreamlike idealism in her story that "calls for truth and equity" but also creates "glamour of beauty and romance" enough to hide the flaws of southern life forty years before.[157] Still, *Dem Good Ole Times* is more than a golden memory of earlier days. Written in the wake of the heated rhetoric of the 1902 Constitutional Convention that effectively disfranchised black Virginians, the retrospective vignettes answer charges long leveled at slave owners by abolitionists, from the colonial period through Reconstruction (for example: was there enough food? did slaves experience cruelty? were they allowed to go to church?).

Through the voice of Daddy Ben, who describes the antebellum era to his granddaughter, Mrs. Dooley assures the reader that all was well and good: "Dar nuver wux de time, on dat plantashun, when you couldn'n hyur sombordy laughin un singing, un dar wuz always some kind a frolic on han. . . . Dar wuz health un happiness evywhar. At de house twuz dinners, un suppers, un drivin, un ridin, un de young ladies walkin bout, wid de gempmun joying uv deyself. Look like de birds in de trees war no happier den we all."[158] Old Ben testifies to his past loyalty and satisfaction, recalling that he refused an offer of freedom after saving his owner's child from snakebite. He asked, "Marster, what is we done, dat you should cas us off dis a way? . . . We wants to wick fur you, long is we live, un, please Gord, arter we die, we hopes to be wid you in Heben." In postemancipation Virginia, the old man mourns the loss of a protective slave system, pointing to the grim circumstances of present-day blacks who "strut bout" with empty stomachs and all their meager possessions on their backs. Most of all, he regrets that his granddaughter "ay noth'n but a po little free nigger, dat nuver had de pledgers, we all wuz use to, when we wuz chillun." Equating freedom with a loss of identity, the little girl indignantly responds, "I ay no sich a thing. I's Miss Mary's maid, dat un noth'n else."[159]

Oral history offers a dynamic alternative viewpoint of a domestic worker who envisions much more than being a servant "un noth'n else." Frances Twiggs Walker, who worked as the Dooleys' head cook after 1919, extended a standing invitation to her niece for weekend visits in her garage apartment at Maymont. Recalling those visits, Virgie Payne remembered her aunt's uniform and duties and the arrangement of the mansion kitchen. She also remembered meeting Sallie Dooley, who told the girl that she hoped she would grow up to be a fine cook like her aunt, as well as Frances Walker's response that "I don't want her to be a cook." Her aunt, she continued, did not try to teach her to cook. Instead, she urged young Virgie in confidence: "You learn something besides cooking, because they'll cook you to death."[160]

The defiant note of Mrs. Walker's answer provides an unsentimental commentary on servant life. As Sallie Dooley looked back to the nineteenth century with sentimentalizing nostalgia, Frances Walker seems to have anticipated new opportunities for education, suffrage, and employment outside of domestic service for African Americans in the twentieth century.

THE GILDED AGE SOUTH

through Photographs

Period images help us envision the separate but parallel experiences of James and Sallie Dooley and the men and women who once served them. Unfortunately, at the presumed directive of Sallie Dooley, most of the couple's personal papers were destroyed following her death in 1925. That critical bonfire, tended by three of Mrs. Dooley's nieces and a former housemaid, may have included existing photographs of Maymont's domestic staff. What follows is a photographic essay comprising related images—primarily Richmond-specific—from the Maymont House Archives and public and private collections.

Maymont House, completed in 1893, sits amidst one hundred acres of rolling parkland on the north bank of the James River. During their residence, 1893–1925, the Dooleys developed the estate by adding an arboretum, picturesque outbuildings, ornamental gardens, fountains, and a waterfall. (Photograph © Richard Cheek)

A Confederate veteran wounded at the Battle of Williamsburg, James Henry Dooley (1841-1922) became a successful attorney and businessman of the New South. In the 1880s and 1890s, he parlayed his intelligence, capital, and luck into a multimillion-dollar fortune. (Maymont Foundation)

Keenly proud of a family lineage descending from colonial Virginia, Sallie May Dooley (1846–1925) grew up near her grandparents' Lunenburg County, Virginia, plantation. She would later idealize the antebellum plantation system in her 1906 novel, *Dem Good Ole Times*. (Maymont Foundation)

The pink drawing room is one of the more formal spaces in the thirty-three-room Maymont mansion. The Dooleys entertained here, with the assistance of their large domestic staff. (Photograph © Richard Cheek)

Main Street, Richmond, Virginia, as it appeared in 1900. The view is from Eleventh Street, looking west, near James Dooley's law office at 1103 East Main. (The Valentine Museum/Richmond History Center)

James R. L. Fitzgerald, Maymont chauffeur, poses behind the wheel of the Dooleys' Winton limousine in 1916. This rare image, along with three others of a uniformed Fitzgerald (see also p. 134), are the only surviving Dooley-era employee photographs. (Maymont Foundation; gift of Mrs. Aurelia Fitzgerald)

The Dooleys' summer home, Swannanoa, was completed in 1913. Described by their cook, Hannah Walker, as a "castle in the sky," the marble-encased mansion sits on a brow atop Afton Mountain near Waynesboro, Virginia. (Maymont Foundation)

Even James Dooley's prestige and wealth could not fully protect his African American employees from the sting of segregationist practices. His 1921 letter describes the refusal of a taxi driver to transport them on the basis of race. (Manuscript Archives, Virginia Historical Society)

Looking out toward the camera with a slight smile, an unidentified housemaid stands behind her seated employers, Mr. and Mrs. John H. Montague, in their Linden Row home. The employee wears the typical afternoon uniform, apron, and cap required of female staff for such duties as serving tea, answering the door, or waiting at the dinner table. (Cook Collection, The Valentine Museum/ Richmond History Center)

The domestic employees of a prominent Richmond household assemble for a group photograph, ca. 1905-1910. Crisp uniforms were the order of the day even during the summer season at their employers' country estate. (Private collection)

For this photograph taken in the drawing room of their East Marshall Street home, ca. 1882, Dr. and Mrs. William B. Gray have included their butler. Was his presence meant to signify the couple's upper-class status or their affection for the unnamed employee? Perhaps it was both. (The Valentine Museum/ Richmond History Center)

Gardeners and a young errand boy join the house staff for this portrait, made about 1910 at an unidentified residence. The seated cook (at center, holding a strainer) likely held seniority. (Cook Collection, The Valentine Museum/Richmond History Center)

Menservants were valued in elite households for such skills as setting a formal table and serving meals *à la Russe*. They also made a livelihood with such fashionable talents in restaurants and private clubs. Here the majordomo and a waiter look over preparations for a banquet at the Westmoreland Club, of which James Dooley was a founding member. (Cook Collection, The Valentine Museum/Richmond History Center)

Sallie Dooley's lady's maid would have assisted her with bathing and dressing and by caring for her wardrobe. As suggested in this studio photograph taken about 1890, upper-class women needed assistance in donning elaborate costumes that closed up the back and had complex drapery, wraps, or trains. (Library of Congress, Prints and Photographs Division, LC-USZ62-100205)

An unknown cook grinds coffee beans in the kitchen of Pratt's Castle, Richmond, ca. 1905. The double-oven range in the background, with its attached hot-water boiler, is similar to the one that once dominated the Maymont House kitchen. (The Valentine Museum/ Richmond History Center)

Although the Dooleys purchased automobiles in the early 1900s, they still maintained their carriages and stable of horses. The Maymont coachman wore a uniform similar to the one pictured in this Richmond photograph, ca. 1890. (The Valentine Museum/Richmond History Center)

Because the Dooleys were childless, they had no need for a nursemaid at Maymont. Nevertheless, child-care providers figured prominently among domestic workers during the Gilded Age. In Richmond white families turned to the black community for midwives, baby nurses (assisting in the first few months after childbirth), and nursemaids. In this studio image "Mammy" Lucy Wood reads to Nellie Meade, ca. 1903. (The Valentine Museum/ Richmond History Center)

In his memoirs James Branch Cabell recalled the daily assemblage of uniformed African American nursemaids in Monroe Park: "These ladies wore white caps and large white aprons, befrilled proudly.... None dared to assail [their] authority." A young Mary "Mate" Branch Converse is pictured in this impromptu gathering, ca. 1914, fourth child from the right. Behind her is "Mammy" Maggie Berry Brown. (Courtesy of Mate B. Converse)

Close bonds between employers and employees could span generations. Twenty-five years after her Monroe Park outings with baby Mate, Maggie Berry Brown assisted with the care of Mrs. Converse's infant son, Melville, in 1939. (Courtesy of Mate B. Converse)

Laundresses made up the highest percentage of working women in Richmond in the late nineteenth and early twentieth centuries. Their work was physically demanding, requiring hours of lifting, bending, and scrubbing against a washboard like the one pictured before an unidentified laundress here. (Library of Congress, Prints and Photographs Division, LC-USZ62-118922)

As part of domestic-science curricula in public and private schools, African American girls were taught such skills as cooking, cleaning, sewing, and child care. Uniformed students gather around a coal-burning range in Virginia Randolph's cooking class, Henrico County Industrial School, ca. 1910–1920. (Jackson Davis Papers, no. 3072. The Albert and Shirley Small Special Collections Library, University of Virginia Library)

While the majority of African American Richmonders resided in Jackson Ward, there were a number of black communities throughout the city, including Shockoe Hill, Navy Hill, New Town, Penitentiary Bottom, Randolph, and sections of Church Hill and Fulton. Many of these neighborhoods lacked municipal services, yards, sidewalks, and paved streets. This view depicts the 1800 block of Rosewood Avenue near Maymont. (Charles Louis Knight, *Negro Housing in Certain Virginia Cities* [Richmond, 1927], p. 47. Library of Virginia)

Saint Luke Penny Savings Bank was located at First and Marshall Streets in Richmond's historic Jackson Ward. Maggie Lena Walker, its president, was the first female to found a bank in the United States. (Richmond Postcard Collection, Special Collections and Archives, James Branch Cabell Library, Virginia Commonwealth University)

In 1905, decades after the end of slavery, African Americans parade in downtown Richmond in celebration of Emancipation Day. (Library of Congress, Prints and Photographs Division, LC-D401-18421)

St. James Gilpin was the proprietor of this boot and shoe store at 506 E. Broad. His was among several black-owned businesses in Gilded Age Richmond. (Library of Congress, Prints and Photographs Division, LC-USZ62-99053)

Black churches and benevolent societies in Richmond sponsored excursions into the countryside. Dressed in Sunday best, young people pause for a photograph in the 1880s. How many among them were maids, butlers, coachmen, or cooks, enjoying an afternoon off? (Cook Collection, The Valentine Museum/Richmond History Center)

Jesus Died for Both, a lithographic print, once hung in the home of William Dilworth, Maymont head butler 1919–1925. It presented a vision of racial equality, if not on earth during strict segregation then later in heaven. (Maymont Foundation; gift of Harold P. Bailey)

Many descendants and friends of former Dooley employees visit Maymont House, which is open to the public as a house museum. Pictured (left to right) are double descendants: Sylvester Walker and his cousins Doris Walker Woodson and John W. Walker. They have shared photos of and information about their grandmother, Frances Twiggs Walker, and their respective parents, John Thomas Walker and Frances Walker. They were among approximately 150 Twiggs-Walker-Smith descendants who gathered at Maymont for a family reunion in 2001. (Maymont Foundation)

As funding permits, Maymont Foundation is carefully restoring the mansion's service spaces to their original appearance. Oral histories and period photographs have helped shape the acquisition of appropriate furnishings and artifacts. This artist's rendering approximates the appearance of the Maymont kitchen, ca. 1910. (Maymont Foundation)

omestic employees left little behind to document their lives and labors in the Gilded Age. Most of the household literature of the period was written by and for the middle class and rarely takes into account the workers' point of view. The era's Progressive movement, however, produced a handful of reformers and social scientists who probed the difficulties of the "Servant Problem" through investigations, surveys, and interviews.[1] As a result, studies such as Lucy Salmon's *Domestic Service* (1897) and, at the other end of the Maymont period, *The Negro in Richmond, Virginia* (1929) by the Richmond Council of Social Agencies document invaluable information about household work and workers. In publishing quotations from servant interviews, they also gave voice to a traditionally silent workforce. Closer to our own time, scholars including Judith Rollins, Elizabeth Clark-Lewis, and Tera Hunter have gathered data and oral histories from a rapidly fading generation of cooks, butlers, maids, and laundresses—all manner of "help" from the early years of the twentieth century. To these resources we add our own rare snippets of Maymont and Richmond memories in an attempt to reconstruct the employees' perspective.

From Morning to Night

The grand door on the west facade of Maymont is the ceremonial entrance into the mansion. Its large cast-iron door knocker is engraved: "FAITH SHUTS THE DOOR AT NIGHT AND MERCY OPENS IT IN THE MORNING." The inscription evokes the hope of one's passing the night safely and, with the grace of God, awakening to another day. In thinking of domestic service at Maymont, we might—with an apologetic smile—reword the inscription: "The butler shuts the door at night and the housemaid opens it in the morning." The beauty, order, and even security of the mansion were due in part to the employees who worked there. In re-creating the typical day-to-day routine of the people of Maymont—the Dooleys and their staff—we can imagine the many instances of faith and mercy required on both sides to keep the household running smoothly.

In general, domestic service was labor intensive, requiring individuals to run up and down stairs, lift, scrub, and bend hour after hour. It also demanded that the workers use their powers of perception, anticipation, and diplomacy as they went about their tasks. Their work unfolded in a whirlwind of daily tasks, weekly chores, and monthly or seasonal chores. All along, persistent demands kept household employees working from morning to night.

A hypothetical day at Maymont might unfold in the following manner. Before the Dooleys rose, their live-in staff awoke, dressed, and began their workday about 6:30 A.M. Within the next hour, live-out employees arrived, coming down the service road and into the basement-level back entrance. On the first floor, the housemaid and the second butler straightened, dusted, and swept. In cooler months, the second butler would have also made the first of many visits of the day to the furnace in the basement to ensure that it had a sufficient amount of coal.

The head butler laid the table in the dining room or second-floor morning room and consulted with the kitchen staff either in person or through the speaking tube in the butler's pantry. In the basement, the cook and her assistant fired up the double-oven kitchen range. In half an hour the coals were hot enough to prepare breakfast. At the same time the cook reviewed the day's menu, previously approved by Sallie Dooley. Having made an inventory of the contents of the pantry, cold room, and icebox, she noted food supplies needed from the market. The list would be sent via the coachman or chauffeur for pickup or called in by telephone for delivery to the house. On occasion James Dooley himself would stop by the market to pick up groceries for his family and staff.[2] Upstairs, the lady's maid and second butler answered separate summonses to assist Major and Mrs. Dooley with bathing and dressing. On request, either would attend the couple if they preferred breakfast in their rooms. Downstairs, after the

Dooleys had eaten, the staff gathered at the oak table in the kitchen to have their own breakfast and discuss the news of the day.

The butler cleared the dishes from the upstairs morning room, carried them down a flight, and washed them in the butler's pantry. In the kitchen, the cook's assistant cleaned pots, pans, and staff dishes. The second butler swept the front and side porches and steps, and the chauffeur washed the Packard limousine and brought it around to transport Major Dooley the two miles to his office at the Merchant's National Bank building downtown. The butler awaited a summons on the annunciator (bell box) by Mrs. Dooley, who would apprise him of her day's schedule and tell him whether company would be coming to the mansion. He then began setting up for luncheon or tea. The second butler or housemaid assisted him as needed.

Throughout the late morning and afternoon, the house hummed with activity. Upstairs, the housemaid aired, straightened, and cleaned the Dooleys' bedrooms and bathrooms. The lady's maid tidied clothes in the wardrobe and sorted out garments and linens for special mending and cleaning. Downstairs, the butler polished silver, surveyed household supplies and foodstuffs in his pantry, and went to the basement to check the inventory of the wine cellar. Below stairs, the cook prepared lunch (called "dinner" by southerners in this era) for Mrs. Dooley and any guests, which was sent up by dumbwaiter and served by the butlers in the dining room at noon. On weekdays, James Dooley likely would have eaten lunch in a restaurant or at his club, near his office. Sunday dinners, served sometime in the afternoon between 1:00 and 3:00 P.M., were heavier meals consisting of more courses and special kinds and cuts of meat and fish. Friends and family members would frequently be invited to Sunday dinner—adding to the day's demand for greater quality and quantity of food and service.

At Maymont the staff partook of its own midday meal after the Dooleys were served, likely interrupted by rings from the annunciator, summonses through the speaking tube, and deliveries of coal, ice, flowers, and groceries at the service door. While meals had some similarities to those served upstairs, there were also differences. The cook would have varied the menu to better suit African American foodways—for instance, substituting greens for spinach. Oral history also suggests that the Dooleys provided lesser cuts of meats for the employees' table. If pork tenderloin was served abovestairs, pork chops were the likely entrée below.[3]

Each Monday, the laundress undertook the week's washing in the basement laundry. While she could enjoy the convenience of running water, there were probably no electrical appliances to aid her work. The laundry may have been outfitted with a manual washing machine, with interior spokes that rotated as the laundress cranked or pumped an exterior lever. More likely, she rubbed each article against a washboard in the laundry's triple-unit tubs, rinsed it, and ran it through a hand wringer. She then hung it on lines and racks, both inside and out, to dry. During the following day or two, she returned to press the garments and linens with flatirons heated on the laundry stove. Mondays, Wednesdays, and Saturdays, the kitchen staff baked bread. (While commercial bakeries were abundant in Richmond, upper-class families strove to avoid the embarrassment of having "bought-bread" on their tables.) Fridays were set aside for deep cleaning chores such as rug beating and extensive dusting, sweeping, and mopping. And every day brought an endless parade of silver—small spoons to oversize urns—in need of polishing.[4]

Evening meals above stairs ranged from light suppers to fancy dinners depending on the Dooleys' schedule. Table and dining-room preparation varied accordingly. Elaborate dinner parties required the butler, second butler, and maid to place linens, china, silver, and crystal hours ahead. During the meal, the head butler coordinated the timing and arrival of each course with the kitchen staff in order to ensure its proper temperature and presentation. Larger meals required employees to bring trays up the service stairs and elevator in addition to using the small, hand-operated dumbwaiter. Dressed in formal attire, the butler and second butler served and removed dishes and, afterwards, cleared the table. Once the Dooleys and their guests retired to the drawing room and library, the employees ate their supper in the kitchen. As the staff traditionally had Thursday afternoons and alternating Sunday afternoons off, suppers for James and Sallie Dooley on these days would be light fare, prepared earlier. Employees rotated afternoons away so that at least one worker would be available to wait at table.

Later in the evening, the butler served light refreshments to the Dooleys and their guests. Tidying the butler's pantry, he washed and put away the dishes. Below stairs, the kitchen staff put away food supplies, washed dishes, scoured pans, and laid out equipment for the morning. The cook's assistant cleaned the ashes out of the range and placed paper twists and kindling for the next morning's fire. Upstairs, in her employer's bedrooms, the housemaid turned down bedclothes and set out small pitchers of fresh water and drinking glasses for nighttime sipping. Later, the lady's maid and second butler helped the Dooleys undress and attended to any of their needs for the night. The live-in staff checked the furnace, turned off the lights, secured the house, and retired to their rooms to bathe, read, and rest—always with the understanding that the call box could ring for them in the night. In the meantime, live-out workers made their way home, a few yards down the service road or several miles away by foot and streetcar. Before another day dawned, they enjoyed the company and served the needs of their own families.

From Slavery to Waged Labor

Following emancipation, African Americans in the South sought economic self-sufficiency. Communal networks such as families, churches, and benevolent and secret societies helped many make the crucial transition from mere survival to stability. Life was precarious for black southerners, whose standards of living remained far beneath those of white people from the same economic level. Dilapidated housing, poor sanitation, inadequate health care, and low and irregular income contributed to a high rate of sickness and death. In the years between 1907 and 1927, the average life expectancy of an African American living in Richmond was thirty-seven years, compared to fifty-two years for a white resident.[5]

In urban centers such as Richmond, a small percentage of African Americans achieved middle-class status—among them teachers, lawyers, doctors, businessmen, and ministers. Most black wage earners, however, struggled with poor education, limited job training and opportunities, and racial discrimination at every turn. As a result, they comprised a permanent sector of the working class who made their way on subsistence wages from unskilled or semiskilled jobs.[6]

In seeking employment in the postemancipation years, black men generally retreated from domestic labor. Renouncing "women's work," they looked for jobs in flour mills, ironworks, and tobacco plants or as independent tradesmen such as carpenters, barbers, and shoemakers. If they remained in service, men tended to prefer work in public spaces such as hotels and restaurants, as waiters, porters, and cooks. African American women, doubly disadvantaged by race and gender, found their job opportunities extremely limited. Shop, office, and most manufactory work was all but closed to them. In Richmond many female laborers did secure low-paying jobs as stemmers in tobacco factories. The majority, however, found waged employment in private households as cooks, maids, nursemaids, and—primarily—as maids-of-all-work. Working within their own homes, they also earned a livelihood as laundresses and seamstresses.[7]

Few working-class jobs could provide a living wage for a household. Problems with unemployment and seasonal layoffs made it necessary for all capable family members to work and pool their resources as an economic unit. Supporting families at the margin of survival, many more black daughters, wives, and mothers worked than did white ones. Clarrsia Agee, the youngest of ten children, was sent from the country in 1916 to work as a maid in Richmond. She recalled that her wages of $4 a week seemed like "a lot of money." Half, she noted, would go home to support her parents in Goochland County. After setting aside an amount for the streetcar and odd expenses, Mrs. Agee deposited the remainder in a savings account at the Saint Luke Penny Savings Bank.[8]

A wife's or daughter's wages from domestic work were often the crucial and sometimes the sole contribution to the family income. In 1901 Orra Langhorne noted a lack of understanding on the part of employers concerning the economic burden shouldered by their household workers. "The negro mother of to-day who goes into service," she wrote, "has to pay house rent, as few employers will tolerate negro children about the kitchen. . . . Her family must be supplied with fuel, and they as well as herself must be clothed. The sick must be cared for. And the fund for all these needs is the woman's wages, usually from one to two dollars per week."[9] One husband, laid off from his work as a brick mason, explained the importance of his wife's work as a laundress: "that dollar a week she gets for it comes in mighty handy when I'm out of work. A dollar's worth of flour or meal will keep you from going hungry for a long time when you're out hunting for a job." In 1916 E. Azalia Hackley paid homage to the women who earned a living and raised a family at the same time: "No one should ever scorn a colored working woman," she wrote. "She has been the bone and sinew of the race."[10]

In the postbellum South, employers and workers alike sought to understand and negotiate domestic service within a free-labor context. Terms of employment were typically verbal and frustratingly fluid. Employers could withhold payment or let a worker go at any time, and employees could leave for a potentially better placement with little or no notice. A few individuals, like Lucy Holladay in Spotsylvania County, Virginia, crafted homemade contracts with their waged help. To secure a maid-of-all-work at her estate, Prospect Hill, Mrs. Holladay drew up an agreement in 1888 with Laura Coleman, the mother of a potential employee. According to the document, young Izzie Coleman would serve as a live-in domestic for a full year, after which time her mother would receive $10. "She is to do any kind of work of which she is capable, when required by Mrs. Holladay," the document reads. If the girl disobeyed or left the premises without permission, it continues, she and her mother would forfeit the year's payment. The final stipulation states that "Mrs. Holladay is to find Izzie's provision of food and Laura Coleman is to find her clothing and bedclothes." The economic imperative forcing mother to part with child was likely great. Alongside the year's wages, amounting to $190 in today's money, the Coleman household would gain the funds that otherwise would have gone toward Izzie's care and feeding. The mother may have also reasoned that her daughter would come away with skills for future employment. Whereas the contract clearly articulates the employer's expectations and needs, it gives no hint of Laura Coleman's thoughts and rationale. Her single "X" at the bottom indicates her consent to sending her daughter forth into the working world.[11]

For African American women, racial, gender, and class barriers left few economic recourses to domestic work. "There wasn't anything but housework," recalled Mary Atkins Anderson, who as a teenager came in from rural Henrico County to work as a live-in nursemaid with a Byrd Park family. Doris Walker Woodson, whose mother and grandmother—as well as several aunts and uncles—served as household employees at

Maymont, described domestic service as a type of economic slavery: "You were free, but you weren't in a sense, because there was not much else to do—that you were allowed to do. Even sometimes with an education, you still had to resort to going back to that kind of work, something menial." In his 1901 leaflet, "Careers Open to Young Negro-Americans," W. E. B. Du Bois cited federal census statistics showing the predominance of domestic service as an occupation among the nation's working black women, second only to farm labor. Du Bois, a Harvard-trained black sociologist and activist, noted such advantages of domestic work as the attainment of skilled homemaking techniques and job security due to unlimited demand. The list of disadvantages was short but daunting: "Social stigma, long hours, low wages, limited advancement." In another assessment, Du Bois correlated the difficulties of domestic work with the legacy of slavery, the inextricable linking of "a despised race to a despised calling."[12]

In his *Theory of the Leisure Class*, Thorstein Veblen connected the persistent disrepute of domestic service with growing class distinctions. "We have a realising sense of ceremonial uncleanness ... associated in our habits of thought with menial service," he writes. "It is felt by all persons of refined taste that a spiritual contamination is inseparable from certain offices that are conventionally required of servants." Without question, domestic workers were hired to perform menial tasks deemed too unpleasant, too tedious, too strenuous, or too demeaning for their upper- and middle-class employers. In short, as historian Phyllis Palmer points out, "the wife's cleanliness was made possible by the domestic's dirtiness."[13] The routine duties of domestic servants were labor-intensive and arduous. Workers endured long hours on their feet—or their hands and knees—as they dusted, swept, cleaned, and polished. They removed trash, scrubbed bathrooms, changed sheets, and collected soiled clothing and linens. Immersing their hands in hot water with caustic cleaners, they wiped down walls, counters, and floors. And in this era no one dared to announce that she or he didn't "do windows."

Less physical duties such as cooking and serving also took their toll. For a few summers during her teenage years, Doris Woodson served as an assistant to her mother, Frances Walker, former Maymont cook. Ms. Woodson recalled the tedious routine of food preparation and service in an upper-class household: "[Our employers] had gourmet meals, with so many courses. It took all day, from morning to dinnertime, to cook *one* meal. It took them 2 to 2$^{1}/_{2}$ hours or more to eat a meal. You never got out of the kitchen before 10:00 or 10:30 at night. Washing dishes: You had a thousand dishes—a dish for everything, a piece of eating utensil for every, single different thing. So it was a long, drawn-out process." The next day, it all began again.[14]

The effects of long hours and a heavy workload could be eased or worsened by the quality of the daily relationship with one's employer. In the postemancipation South this connection was being redefined, household by household, with uneven results. Whatever the association between the person who hired, directed, paid, and fired employees and the worker who treaded the thin boundary of being "in the family, but not *of it*," the fundamental nature of the relationship remained economic. In his 1901 *Marrow of Tradition*, African American novelist Charles Chesnutt suggests that a new generation of workers had few illusions about this essential point. In the story, a young nursemaid observes the conspicuous deference that the older Mammy Jane gives to the family that once enslaved her: "These old-time negroes, she said to herself, made her sick with their slavering over the white folks, who, she supposed, favored them and made much of them because they had once belonged to them,—much the same reason why they fondled their cats and dogs. For her own part, they gave her nothing but her own wages, and small wages at that, and she owed them nothing more than equivalent service. It was purely a matter of business; she sold her time for their money. There was no question of love between them."[15]

Doris Woodson, a descendant of two generations of Dooley employees, reflected on the various working relationships between server and served in early twentieth-century households. "A lot of the African-American workers—the servants—were deferential to their employers in order to get favors," she commented. "You'd hear them talk about that. In fact, [that practice developed] in slavery. In general, a lot of times the Negro was deferential to the white man to be treated in a special way. And they talked about it and laughed about it behind their backs." Ms. Woodson, however, cautioned that it is impossible to make generalizations about all employee-employer relationships. These varied from person to person, household to household. "People had individual temperaments. Some were more sensitive and caring; some people were just more cold and aloof."[16]

Efforts by African Americans to break away from domestic service met with resistance if they infringed on traditionally white jobs. Concerned that black women might abandon private household employment for jobs in restaurants and stores, the Housewives' League of Richmond launched a preemptive strike in 1919. A committee of five prominent women called on the city's Retail Merchants' Association to request a "substitution of white girls for the colored maids now employed as waitresses and in other capacities in order that the Negroes may be released for domestic service." The *People's Pilot*, a local African American newspaper, printed the response from the Merchants' Association to a letter of concern from the Richmond chapter of the NAACP. "We have no control over the actions in our stores in our membership regarding their employers," the association's secretary assured. "My personal opinion is that you and your associates need not be alarmed, for there is not quite enough help to 'go' round. The whole industrial fabric of our nation is in a state of readjustment and will before long be satisfactorily worked out I am sure." While cheering the association, the magazine's editor wondered: "Why should colored citizens be forever consigned to one particular branch of menial service? . . . What in the world is the matter with some of the members of that 'League?' What will they do next?"[17]

Difficult Work in a Difficult Era

It wasn't difficult for the Reverend Joseph Carter Jr., son of former Maymont butler Joseph Carter Sr., to recall the de jure and de facto segregation in early twentieth-century Richmond: "We were living through it. If your eyes were open and your ears were open, you couldn't escape it." His wife, Mildred Morton Carter, who was born and spent most of her adult life on Clay Street in Richmond's Jackson Ward, pointed to the frustrations of public transportation. "If the streetcar was empty," she recalled, "blacks could sit near the front. But as white people began to get on the car, we would have to—even though we paid for a seat—move to the back. And any number of times—more than I can count—I've had the streetcar conductor *stop* the car and ask us to get up and give white people our seats." Mrs. Carter continued: "Sometimes there'd be black people [on the streetcar], who'd worked all day, standing. I would notice black men who'd been out in the Westhampton area mowing the lawn in the summer— hot, sweaty, tired, no place to wash. And then, when they'd get on the trolley—it was the only way to get home—the white ladies would be looking at them with their noses turned up because they smelled bad. That used to bug me, I won't lie to you."[18]

In the face of segregation, however, African American Richmonders established a thriving community. Jackson Ward—with its banks, businesses, restaurants, theaters, and churches—became the heart of a growing black consciousness. Community leaders developed and espoused a pragmatic philosophy. Maggie Lena Walker, daughter of a laundress and the first woman to found a bank in the United States, stressed social uplift, the dignity of honest labor, and the importance of saving. (Laundresses numbered significantly among investors at her Saint Luke Penny Savings Bank.)[19] "Labor, all labor is noble and holy," wrote Daniel Webster Davis, Richmond's well-known writer, minister, and educator. The *Richmond Planet*, the city's leading African American newspaper, encouraged its readers: "We cannot reach the top of the ladder at one bound. Bow low, and work! 'Stoop to conquer.' You do the stooping, and your children will do the conquering."[20]

To "bow low and work" was a strategy of accommodation and survival in an age of growing racial oppression and violence. At the workplace and on the street, African Americans guarded their words and actions. They also learned to assume a humble, unassertive demeanor in the presence of whites. Domestic workers especially understood that a deferential behavior in the presence of "Miz Ann" and "Mr. Charlie"—meaning the universal white employer—was an unwritten requirement of employment. Walter Bernard Whiting—whose grandfather Winston Edmunds served as head butler to twelve of Virginia's governors—reflected on the sometimes unequal results of that deference: "The white, upper-class employers, like the Dooleys, had a sense that the workers 'belonged' to them. The workers, in turn, gave the impression: 'I am completely satisfied here.' That attitude was part of the job. Choices were few. One could leave. Some workers had an ingratiating attitude, like 'Uncle Tom,' but they also had clothes on their backs. At the same time, some folks worked as hard as they could work—and did not succeed."[21]

Audrey Smith entered household service at age twelve, having learned the expected demeanor from her mother, Georgia Anderson—lady's maid to Sallie Dooley. "Even when we were serving, you made yourself as inconspicuous as possible," she recalled. "No fraternizing or smiling, or anything. You went to do your work. You couldn't get out of your place. You had a place to stay, and that was your place." In thinking of the African American employees in her childhood home, Cleiland Donnan had no recollection of overt expressions of bitterness or frustration. "When you're not treated right or fairly, you're bound to feel something," she reflected. "If they had any feelings of resentment, it did not come out. . . . What our black servants had to bear in their hearts is beyond my imagination, because I don't know service like that."[22]

W. E. B. Du Bois described this assumption of deference or invisibility as a protective veil that covers the real self.[23] Others, like poet Paul Laurence Dunbar, likened it to a mask:

> We wear the mask that grins and lies,
> It hides our cheeks and shades our eyes,—
> This debit we pay to human guile;
> With torn and bleeding hearts we smile,
> And mouth with myriad subtleties.
> Why should the world be over-wise,
> In counting all our tears and sighs?
> Nay let them only see us, while
> We wear the mask.[24]

In Richmond, one man's violation of the racial code had an unexpected outcome. In 1899 Murphy's Hotel, a grand facility for white guests only, hosted John L. Sullivan, the famous former heavyweight boxing champion of the world. One morning the boxer used a racial slur and threatened the black waiter, William Miller, who was serving him breakfast. In retaliation, Miller knocked him out with a coffeepot. After taking a hasty "vacation" at the hotel's insistence, Miller returned to find himself a hero. When his story appeared in the *Richmond Times*, financial contributions poured in from black and white admirers. William Royall, the newspaper's chief editorial writer, presented him with three thousand dollars and a silver coffeepot, inscribed: "To the World's Champion Coffee Pot Fighter." With his windfall, the former waiter opened Miller's Hotel for Negro Patrons.[25]

Typically, however, African Americans were not rewarded for breaking the "racial etiquette" of the Jim Crow era. Instead, they reaped unhappy consequences ranging from a stiff dressing down and docking of pay to the loss of a job or violence. There was little recourse in the workplace. Short of quitting, household employees could act out frustrations in indirect ways, such as work slowdowns or absenteeism. Nevertheless, economic necessity required domestics to "go along to get along" in a system that demanded unquestioning compliance. In an editorial, *Richmond Planet* editor John Mitchell cautioned readers: "Be respectful to white people, colored folks. Teach your children to be polite and obliging to them. We're right now in the midst of a world's struggle and we need their friendship, just as much as they need our help."[26]

After serving as Maymont's butler, Joseph Carter Sr. enlisted in the army during World War I. On his return to Richmond, he worked as a laborer in a tobacco warehouse for many years. When this work dwindled in the depression, Joseph Carter Jr. recalled, he took up odd jobs, including setting up pins in a bowling alley. "The people he was working for and the people that were playing would sometimes try to hit him with the ball. He would be trying to set the pins up and keep out of their way too." Reverend Carter continued, "He believed in work—going to work. Sometimes he would share with me the fact that work might not have always been pleasant. . . . He said, 'Sometimes, when I'm working, your Daddy is not really your Daddy. You have to do what you have to do to bring the paycheck home.' It wasn't always something he would have done if he had his druthers."[27]

Despite the challenges and difficulties of working in low-status occupations, black workers—of whom domestic employees made up a large percentage—persevered. Their courage and sacrifices did not go unnoticed or unappreciated. Of her grandparents, one African American woman wrote: "while Jim Crow played like a background Muzak unlistened to [they] went purposefully in and out the front door of their life." Writer James Baldwin declared: "I have great respect for that unsung army of black men and women who trudged down back lanes and entered back doors, saying 'Yes, Sir' and 'No, Ma'am.' . . . They did not like saying 'Yes, Sir,' and 'No Ma'am' but . . . [they] knew that the job had to be done, and they put their pride in their pockets in order to do it. It is very hard to believe that they were in any way inferior to the white men and women who opened those back doors."[28]

Many domestic workers transcended the difficult work in a difficult era. Hylah Wright recalled that she did not let the restrictions of the period or the fact that she worked as a domestic deter her: "You came from a decent family, you knew the rules, you just didn't let it bother you." Many workers perceived and used their labors as a vehicle toward a better life— if not for themselves, then for their children. Georgia Anderson, lady's maid to Mrs. Dooley in the 1920s, was eventually able to send her foster daughter, Ruby Childs, to Virginia Union University. Mrs. Childs, now a retired schoolteacher, described her mother's determination and "strong personality," recalling, "Mother passed on to me so many qualities. So many. How to conduct myself as a lady. . . . How to be the best I can be."[29]

Dorothy Cowling, a retired professor from Virginia Union University, earned tuition money by doing domestic work in Virginia State dormitories during holidays. When her classmates asked how she could bear it, she responded: "I didn't come here to major in bathroom stuff. This is helping me to get out of bathroom stuff." Summarizing the experience years later, Dr. Cowling noted, "All work is dignified if indeed you need it to accomplish something. . . . You looked at labor as a job; you accepted it as a way to move on."[30]

Frances Jones, great-granddaughter of Frances Twiggs Walker and granddaughter of Hannah Walker Kenney (head cook and second cook at Maymont, circa 1919–1925), recalled that her forebears emphasized the nobility of labor. "It was hard but honest work," she said. "No one felt belittled by what they did. They did it well. They would tell the young people: 'It is no disgrace to serve. It is an art.'" Nevertheless, Mrs. Jones recalled that her grandmother—in whose home she was raised—also emphasized the importance of education. For the younger generation, she dreamed of opportunities beyond domestic service. Hannah, she recalled, told her: "The only toilet I want you to clean is your own. The only floor I want you to scrub is your own." Hannah Kenney also imparted the importance of voting to her grandchildren. Although women had gained the vote in 1920, black women—like most black men—could not exercise the right until civil- and voting-rights reforms of the 1950s and 1960s. In the Kenney household in Jackson Ward, voting was perceived as a special, almost sacred ritual. "Nana first voted in the 1960 election. At that time, and for elections to follow, she took me along to the polls. My grandmother and mother would dress up to cast their votes at Baker School. People stood in long lines." Hannah Kenney told her: "Always vote." Mrs. Jones added, "I always have."[31]

Terms of Address

In describing their occupations, workers during the Maymont era may have said they were "in service" but would not likely have referred to themselves as "servants." American domestics—white and black—generally rejected the title of "servant," long tainted with the stigma of caste and personal subjugation. At the turn of the century, Eliza Turner, president of the Philadelphia Working-Woman's Guild, stated: "The very words, 'service' and 'servant,' are hateful. It is all well enough to talk about service being divine, but that is not the way the world looks at it." Lillian Pettengill, documenting her experiences as a housemaid in 1903, took exception to the word as well: "A domestic tradeswoman I am, a chamber-maid, a waitress, an employee with an employer, but a servant with a mistress— never, I am an American."[32]

Over the past seventy years that she has been employed as a cook, Richmonder Hylah Wright has found the word "servant" objectionable: "I don't like it, and never have. But there wasn't anything I could do about it." She tried not to let the title bother her when it was in frequent use in the early decades of the twentieth century. Noting that it fell out of fashion for other terms, she said, "it never should have started. . . . 'Servant' is all together different; it even sounds different." Over the years, she referred to herself variously as "maid" or "cook"—precise titles associated with her duties.[33]

Using general terms such as "help" or "domestic" or specific titles such as "cook," "butler," or "maid" helped ameliorate the lingering stigma associated with both title and work. "Servant" may have other inferences as well. For instance, after compiling numerous oral histories of former domestic employees in the Washington, D.C., area, historian Elizabeth Clark-Lewis determined that for some workers, the title "servant" signified live-in status.[34]

Joseph Carter Jr. described an unusual act of linguistic selection and authority in his family. As a child, he resided with his parents—Joseph Carter Sr. (butler at Maymont, 1913–1915) and Sarah Steward Carter—in the P Street home of his maternal grandfather, Otway Steward. He was told that after emancipation from slavery, his grandfather was given the choice of taking his former owner's last name or choosing a new one. He decided on "Steward," Reverend Carter stated, because "he wanted to be in service to his people." Otway Steward lived up to the promise of his chosen name, serving African American Richmond as an educator, artisan, and coeditor of the *Virginia Star,* an early black newspaper.[35]

African Americans were also acutely aware of white linguistic practices that dispensed with their last names, labeled them "Uncle" or "Auntie," or denied them respectful prefixes.[36] As part of a delegation to the governor's office, bank president Maggie Lena Walker found herself addressed by white officials as "Maggie." Through carefully chosen words and deliberate inflection, she commanded attention to the slight and was "Mrs. Walker" by meeting's end. Members of the African American community took care—on the job and at home—to refer to their neighbors and acquaintances as "Mister," "Missus," and "Miss." In large domestic staffs, this was particularly the case with senior staff members. In the 1920s, for example, Maymont staff members may have addressed the head cook and butler as "Mrs. Walker" and "Mr. Dilworth." (As noted earlier, James Dooley once instructed an outside visitor to refer to his head butler as "*Mr. Dilworth.*") At the same time, familiarity and affection could serve as great levelers among coworkers. In thinking of her mother, Georgia Anderson, and her peers on the Maymont staff, Audrey Smith noted, "There was no Mr. or Mrs. It was bad enough to say it to the white people. They called each other 'Georgia,' 'Fannie,' or 'James.'"[37]

Uniforms

If, for employers, a liveried servant was a valued sign of high social status, employees had mixed feelings about dress requirements. Hylah Wright, longtime cook for the Anderson family, fondly remembered the special fabric and cut of particular uniforms that her employer, Isabel Scott Anderson, provided when she was a young maid: "high collar, black satin, cute waistline, white cap all ruffled . . . it was all lace. I recall a pretty black apron she had made. She said she saw it in New York, in a movie. . . . She sent me to a dressmaker and had them made." Mrs. Wright described her daytime working costume as "a pretty blue uniform, with a pretty white apron, and a pretty white [cap] here." For evenings, she wore a "real formal" black-and-white uniform. Richmonder Clarrsia Agee, whose long career as an upstairs maid spanned seven decades, also has warm recollections of her working wardrobe. On one occasion her employer purchased twenty-five dollars worth of white lace to accent her young maid's collars and cuffs. "They all said I was a beautiful lady," she recalled. "And my uniform was lovely."[38]

In elite homes, including Maymont, employers not only required livery but also expected their staff to wear different uniforms for different tasks or times of day. As mentioned previously, the Dooleys supplied their maids with gray, black, and burgundy uniforms with white caps and aprons. The maid would have donned the gray costume for morning and early afternoon cleaning chores. If she was asked to replace or assist the butlers with serving tea or waiting at table in the evening, she would have changed to the more formal black-and-white uniform—or burgundy for special events. The lady's maid would have worn a black uniform, often with a black apron, throughout the day.[39]

Some workers perceived the distinctive costumes as visible symbols of subordination. According to Astor Smith, his grandmother Frances Twiggs Walker had some sensitivity about livery. Family history relates that Mrs. Dooley occasionally required Mrs. Walker, her head cook, to accompany her on errands in her carriage. "She didn't mind that," Mr. Smith noted, "except she did not like to be out in public wearing that uniform." Audrey Smith recalled that employers purchased uniforms for their domestic staff—or, as was the case for her mother, Georgia Anderson, "you could make them and they'd pay for them." Mrs. Anderson, who served as Sallie Dooley's personal maid, had honed her sewing skills in a shirt-making factory in Bowling Green, Virginia. Her daughter recalled that she was a wonderful seamstress, capable of making her own dress patterns. And, when young Audrey went into service as well, her mother designed and made her uniforms out of a special pongee fabric. No matter how fine the fabric or cut, however, the uniform clearly signified a working-class status. At the end of the day, Mrs. Smith noted, "you'd change your clothes before you go, and you'd hang your uniform up. You wore your street clothes home. You didn't come through the streets with your uniform on. That was something we had more pride in. You didn't want nobody to know where you've come from. . . . And when you leave [employment], you leave your uniform. You leave it right there."[40]

In her book *Living In, Living Out*, historian Elizabeth Clark-Lewis documents the recollections of retired day workers who were employed in private households in early twentieth-century Washington, D.C. One individual underscored the overall reluctance of workers to appear in public in domestic-service uniforms. The rejection of livery sometimes extended into the workplace as well. Eventually, the maid began bringing her own work clothes from home. Feeling liberated from the stigma of an employer-imposed costume, she referred to the parcel she carried on her daily commute as her "freedom bag."[41]

"Jesus Died for Both"

Throughout the Maymont era, the church stood at the center of the African American community. "In the South, at least," wrote W. E. B. Du Bois in 1903, "practically every American Negro is a church member. Some to be sure, are not regularly enrolled, and a few do not habitually attend services; but, practically, a proscribed people must have a social centre, and that centre for this people is the Negro church." It was at church, he said, that black Americans found community, comfort, and relief from an unjust world where they were "cut off by color-prejudice and social condition." At the same time, Du Bois expressed concern with the kind of solace the church might offer. The Harvard-trained sociologist pointed out that in order to endure centuries of slavery and more-recent decades of legal and social repression, African Americans tended to focus on heavenly reward rather than struggle for earthly justice. Doctrines of passive submission, humility, and sacrifice, he noted, could foster a resigned fatalism in the long-subordinated race.[42]

Nevertheless, Du Bois recognized that the church provided a crucial safety net for the community. Besides offering spiritual nourishment, black religious institutions provided loans, day care for children and the elderly, medical needs, and job placement. As a case study, he described the archetypal First Baptist congregation in a Virginia town:

> Various organizations meet here,—the church proper, the Sunday-school, two or three insurance societies, women's societies, secret societies, and mass meetings of various kinds. Entertainments, suppers, and lectures are held besides the five or six regular weekly religious services. Considerable sums of money are collected and expended here, employment is found for the idle, strangers are introduced, news is disseminated, and charity distributed. At the same time this social, intellectual and economic centre is the religious centre of great power. . . . The Church often stands as a real conserver of morals, a strengthener of family life, and the final authority on what is Good and Right.[43]

In 1903, when Du Bois was considering the "faith of the fathers," there were twenty-four black churches in Richmond (of which nineteen were Baptist), with approximately 15,400 members.[44] Oral history and extant congregational records indicate that Maymont employees held membership in a number of these churches, both historic and new, several miles distant and close to the estate. These include Leigh Street Methodist, Sixth Mount Zion Baptist, Second Baptist, Fourth Baptist, Fifth Baptist, Moore Street Baptist, and Mount Vernon Baptist Churches.

The household of Joseph Carter Sr., who was employed in the 1910s as a butler at Maymont, had commitments to two churches. His son and namesake, the Reverend Joseph Carter Jr., recalled that his mother was a member of Leigh Street Methodist, while his father attended his childhood church, Fourth Baptist. "He was right there on a Sunday morning, no question about that," he stated. Remembering that the men would often linger out front before services began, he noted that his father knew and greeted everyone. Inside, "We had a particular area in the church where we sat—over on the 28th Street side."[45]

A 1914 study of religious practices among black Virginians marked the impact of domestic employment on church attendance: "People who are employed as cooks or housemaids—people in service—do not 'get off' until Sunday dinner has been served at the homes of their white employers. . . . The evening service is the largest among the Negroes, while it is usually smaller among the whites." William Dilworth, who succeeded Joseph Carter as head butler in the 1920s, was a member of Mount Vernon Baptist on Rosewood Avenue. His daughter, Jeanette Bailey, remarked, "Often on Sundays, he couldn't get there on account of his work, but his money always went there. He would drop it by [a church member's house] on his way to work." On alternating Sunday afternoons, his scheduled time away from Maymont, he could attend evening services with his family.[46]

The descendants of butler William Dilworth recall his fondness for religious imagery, which brought church lessons into the home. Among the various pictures he had on display in his residence on nearby Idlewood Avenue, he cherished a framed illustration titled "Jesus Died for Both."[47] The print, later given by his grandson to Maymont in his honor, depicts Christ blessing both a white and a black child. The image conveys a vision of racial equality—if not on earth during this era of strict segregation, then in heaven.

Training

Many household employees first learned domestic skills at home by helping adults with cleaning, cooking, and child care. Mary Tuck, who was born in 1893 in Mississippi, recalled working as a small child while her parents and siblings picked cotton. "I had to cook, I had to wash, iron, milk the cows, and keep the house clean," she stated. At night, she and her mother did washing and ironing for children boarding at a nearby white high school. When she turned seven, young Mary was sent—like Izzie Coleman—to supplement the family income by working in a white household. She remembered, "I . . . had to get up in a chair to get to the stove."[48]

At the age of twelve, Audrey Smith entered the domestic labor corps in Richmond—sent by her mother to serve tea and clean house for an elderly white woman. "If you were old enough to do something, you had to make money. Because Mama couldn't have no lazy people in the house," Mrs. Smith recalled. Her mother, Georgia Anderson, had found the position through a network of friends. Having mastered domestic skills in various household positions, including her tenure at Maymont as Sallie Dooley's personal maid, Mrs. Anderson taught her daughter the proper way to set a formal table, to serve, to clean, to launder. And she expected results that met her own high standards. Mrs. Smith recalled:

> When Mama told you to iron the napkins, you had to be sure to fold them so that all the corners be even. . . . If you pressed them [crooked] anyway, you had to take it and start all over again. And if she saw any 'cat-faces' in the shirt, you had to dampen it. She told you before, 'Don't *do* that!' If she told you to scrub the floor, and you scrubbed the floor and didn't get into that corner and that corner, you'd say, 'I'm finished.' 'No you're not! Go over again and look in that corner there.' . . . There was no such thing as a mop. You'd get down on your knees to do it.

Following Sallie Dooley's death, Georgia Anderson was hired by the city of Richmond to clean the mansion of her former employer and help show visitors around the renamed "Dooley Museum." To make ends meet, Mrs. Anderson also took in laundry from a handful of out-of-town delegates who relocated to Richmond for General Assembly sessions. She enlisted young Audrey's assistance with washing and ironing. Using the streetcar system, the child also picked up and delivered baskets throughout the city. One day, Mrs. Smith recalled, she hid a basket of clean laundry in the bushes to play at nearby Fountain Lake. The unhappy customer alerted her mother, who in turn gave Audrey a warm reception on her return home. She remembers it as one of her most severe spankings. "You know," Mrs. Smith concluded, "we had no time to play. It was always business, always work."[49]

Many African American children and teenagers also accompanied their mothers, aunts, and older sisters to work for on-the-job training in both chores and interaction with employers. We might assume that Frances Twiggs Walker provided such guidance and training for her family members. During her six- or seven-year tenure at Maymont, her daughters, Hannah, Mary, and Frances, worked sequentially as kitchen maid and her sons Joseph and Abraham were employed as chauffeur, while John Thomas served as butler or second butler. Many of this younger generation of Walkers became gourmet cooks themselves. One daughter, Hannah Walker Kenney, became head cook at Brook Hill for the prestigious Stewart family. Although Frances Walker told Sallie Dooley that she did not want her niece to follow in her vocational footsteps, young Virgie Twiggs served briefly as a second cook under her cousin Hannah at Brook Hill.[50]

The reform impulse of the turn-of-the-century Progressive movement brought attention to the lot of American domestic workers and to their work. Examining the conditions of working women and children, a loose association of settlement-house workers, social scientists, and labor leaders called for the establishment of domestic-service training programs in an attempt to eradicate the stigma of domestic labor and, at the same time, to elevate service occupations. In 1897 Professor Lucy Salmon perceived this solution as beneficial to employer and employee alike. The employer could retain skilled, competent help, she reasoned; the worker, in return, could achieve a higher sense of self-worth as a trained professional. Salmon noted, however, that "the training-school for servants is and must be a failure as long as the class for whom it was founded will not voluntarily attend it in any considerable numbers."[51]

This pragmatic notion of domestic training coincided with Booker T. Washington's well-publicized call for practical education in black schools. In the 1880s he developed a manual training curriculum as founding principal of Tuskegee Normal and Industrial Institute. Believing at the time that African Americans had little choice but to acquiesce to discrimination, Washington espoused racial uplift through economic, not political, means—an accommodationist approach that brought him both the praise of white leaders and condemnation from black civil-rights advocates. "To those of my race who depend on bettering their condition," he urged in his famous speech before the 1895 Atlanta Cotton States Exposition, ". . . I would say: 'Cast down your bucket where you are'. . . . Cast it down in agriculture, mechanics, in commerce, in domestic service, and in the professions. . . . we shall prosper in proportion as we learn to dignify and glorify common labour and put brains and skill into the common occupations of life."[52]

Together, the Progressive reform impulse and Washington's self-help philosophy fueled the development of manual-training curricula in public and private schools for blacks across the South. By the early 1900s Richmond Colored High and Normal School—established following the Civil War by the Freedman's Bureau—offered craft, industrial, and agricultural training courses alongside traditional academic studies. These included domestic-science courses for girls, which focused on the basics of sewing and cooking. After 1908 schools in the surrounding counties benefited from an educational endowment from Anna Jeanes, a Quaker philanthropist from Philadelphia. The Jeanes Fund, earmarked for "industrial training" in rural black schools in the South, paid the salary of a traveling teacher. Virginia Randolph, a young African American educator from Richmond, was named the state's first Jeanes teacher. Keeping a grueling, rotating schedule between twenty-three schools in Henrico County, she submitted a report of her first year's accomplishments that included: "Taught laundry work, sewing, needlework, carpentry and making of shuck mats." Whether they took domestic-sciences courses in the city or the country, students were encouraged to apply their new skills outside the classroom to improve standards of living at home. The training was meant to prepare them for future roles as homemakers, and—if circumstances warranted—for jobs as domestic employees in private residences.[53]

In pursuing higher education, African American women could enroll in home economics courses at Hampton Institute in Hampton and Hartshorn College in Richmond. Supplementing traditional liberal arts programs, domestic science curricula offered instruction in sewing, cooking, and housekeeping. In 1905, for instance, the "Manual Training" requirements for junior-year students at Hampton Institute included "the care of kitchen and kitchen utensils; sweeping and dusting, care of brooms, brushes and dusters; floor-scrubbing; window-cleaning and silver-polishing; care of dining-room, bathroom, and bedroom; care of kerosene lamps; cooking of simple breakfast dishes; table laying; individual breakfast; making of bread."[54]

Richmond's Hartshorn Memorial College, founded in 1883 by Baptist Mission Societies of New England and Michigan, provided high school and college courses for black females. In addition to Latin, physical science, and algebra, Hartshorn offered classes in the "sanitary and housewifely care" of a house, plain sewing, arts of the laundry, plain cooking, principles of caring for the sick, care of clothing, cutting and fitting of plain garments, decorative needlework and knitting, and care of children. During summer breaks, students earned tuition money by working as domestics in private residences in Richmond. A Boston mission society pamphlet quotes a satisfied employer as saying that Hartshorn students were "the best servants we ever had." Hartshorn Memorial College—like Hampton, Tuskegee, and other institutes of higher learning for black Americans—sought not only to educate its students, but also to address "problems of labor and self support." Still, the college's administration insisted that emphasis on "woman's work" did not imply that the school was training domestic servants. Instead, the Hartshorn catalogue explains, such course work prepared each young woman to be "the mother at the head of her own family, and for the teacher or missionary at home or abroad."[55]

Writing from Lynchburg in the late nineteenth century, Orra Langhorne noted the developing educational opportunities for black women. She observed, however, that graduates typically went on to the professions, not service: "The young colored girl . . . on her return from Hampton, Howard, or some institution in the North . . . cannot possibly become a cook, housemaid, or laundress as her mother was before her." Nevertheless, if families of domestic science students fell on hard times, graduates could easily secure service jobs with skills learned at home and at school.[56]

Although such training opportunities existed in Richmond, no records or oral histories indicate that any Maymont employee undertook formal training in domestic skills. Very few black women of the period could afford either the time or the tuition for such programs. According to a survey of Richmond's household employees in the 1920s, the overwhelming majority admitted they had no training before going to work. Rather, the respondents said, their skills were acquired on the job. Emily Brown, who worked as a maid in Richmond in the 1920s, recalled that employers provided training and instruction, and even though they "didn't know how to do it themselves, they could tell you how to do it."[57]

Word of Work

A small percentage of Richmond's domestic workers located jobs through newspaper advertisements or employment agencies. In the last quarter of the nineteenth century, First African Baptist Church on Broad Street served as something of a clearinghouse for employment openings. There, employers could come to meet and interview prospective workers for short- and long-term hires.[58] In 1911 a study of "Women and Labor" by the Richmond YWCA documented four employment agencies in the city, two specializing in domestic service. For placement, the agencies charged the employee between $1 and $1.25 and the employer 25¢ to 50¢. The author of the report, Mrs. R. E. Loving, annotated her listing: "None of these offices appealed to me as being of a very high order."[59]

Most of Richmond's domestic workers found their positions by word of mouth. Hylah Wright entered the employment of the Anderson family when her sister—working for Isabel Anderson's sister—recommended her. Such networking was preferred by employers and employees alike. "They never did like to use the newspaper, because you never knew who you were getting," Mrs. Wright recalled. "You want to really get some good families." Within the tightly woven African American community, with its strong support systems, domestics exchanged information not only about types and availability of jobs but about the reputations of employers as well.[60]

These networks also relayed information about work opportunities outside Richmond and outside Virginia. Some of the grown children of Frances Twiggs Walker migrated north in the 1920s. Most had served with their mother on the staff at Maymont before their relocation. Sylvester Walker, son of John Thomas Walker, describes their move as part of the larger phenomenon of the Great Migration. "During the 1920s–1930s," he noted, "there was a great exodus of blacks from the South for economic purposes. Everyone had hopes that the schools would be better, that there would be . . . more jobs." He described the family support system:

My father migrated to Philadelphia about 1922–23. As his siblings migrated northward, all of them, at one time or another, lived with my father until they could become economically stable. The family was very, very close. Both of my aunts—my Aunt Mary and Aunt Frances, who [earlier] worked at Maymont—lived with my father when they were not working [as live-in cooks]. . . . Generally they were off one or two days a week—Thursday and maybe on a Sunday. Whenever they were off work, they stayed with my father.[61]

The Great Migration, which led half a million African Americans to northern cities in search of better lives and incomes, occurred primarily between 1914 and 1920.[62] The movement, however, began earlier in the late nineteenth century. Writing from Lynchburg, Virginia, Orra Langhorne observed in 1890:

> Wages are very low in the South. . . . This accounts to a great extent for the restlessness of the Negroes. A colored girl who was brisk, cheerful, and efficient was employed in a family near me last winter at $4 per month. Her sister in Philadelphia was earning $4 per week. The latter sent money to pay her younger sister's fare North, having engaged service for her in a nice family. This had quite an unsettling effect upon servants here, and as such cases are constantly occurring there is a steady drain of colored people from Virginia.[63]

In a series of articles between April and August 1917, the *Richmond Planet* examined the "Negro Exodus" and determined that in the South poor educational and work opportunities, increasing violence, and Jim Crow segregation all prompted the "Rush of Negro Workers to the North." The promise of better salaries played no small role in the Great Migration.[64] For more than twenty years, the *Richmond Planet* printed notices from local and out-of-state employment offices looking for workers who would relocate to the North. In 1900 R. W. Elsom at 417 Broad Street, repeatedly advertised: "WANTED WEEKLY 100 COOKS Housemaids and Waitresses for New York and other Northern Cities, wages from $3.00 to $5.00 per week. Transportation furnished."[65] The call for southern black domestics continued over the following two decades. In 1921 D'Antignac's Employment Agency in New York City sought "COLORED HELP WANTED in the NORTH, Laborers and Domestic Servants, In and out of City. Part and Full Time. Phone Audubon 3155."[66]

Following the lead of her Henrico County cousins, Ann Anderson Jones relocated to New York City at age seventeen. "They'd come home to Virginia in their pretty clothes. I didn't know how hard they worked to get them," she recalled. In short time the teenage girl found a position as a live-in maid, but she had difficulty with the job's physical demands. "One of the two ladies there told me, 'where are you from?' I said, 'Virginia.' She said, 'you go back home to your Mama, there. You can't do this work. It is too heavy for you.'" Nevertheless, she stayed on long enough to gain the required reference. Within a year, she had enrolled in nurses' training. Mrs. Jones remembered the strangeness of urban life and a frightening episode in those early weeks up north. One day, she was sent to the roof to hang out laundry. When she began to peg wet clothing to the black cords she found there:

> One of the chauffeurs saw me. He said: 'Hey honey! Don't touch that! Don't you do that, that's electricity! Where'd you come from?' He said, 'You go down there in that lady's house. And you look in that pantry. There's a bag down there. . . . (I don't know why she didn't tell you.) She's got clothespins and a cord . . . you put it on that line.' . . . I was so thankful that man showed me. . . . She thought I knew. I guess that's why she told me to go back to my Mama.[67]

While some young women from the surrounding countryside traveled north for work, the majority found employment in Richmond households with the assistance of family networks—both white and black. In recalling her childhood on Franklin Street, Nancy Lancaster recounted her mother's unusual method of acquiring new domestic help: "She simply raised a front window and asked a passing colored woman if she knew of 'a settled girl' (i.e., one safely married) who might be suitable. Presently an applicant would appear. If she came from Powhatan County, that was in her favor; if she was from Hanover County, that was against her."[68]

After the turn of the century, turnover rates ran high in a market where the demand for servants began to exceed the supply of employees.

Workers felt free to change positions frequently, to the consternation of employers. In her memoirs of Richmond before 1916, Elizabeth Winn recalls when "Mammy Margaret" left her family household for another position: "Father would remonstrate with her for leaving but she would reply that a mole was digging under her foot and when he dug she had to move on." Like all employees, household workers kept an eye and ear toward better circumstances. Leaving or the threat of leaving gave domestics some marginal leverage to improve work conditions and wages.[69]

Living In and Living Out

Forms of domestic employment in the Gilded Age ranged from full-time residential, full-time living out, and part-time to casual hire. Maymont's staff included all variations. A survey of the employee roster between 1920 and 1925, for example, shows the presence of a head butler (living out), second butler (living in), maid (living in), cook (living on the estate), chauffeur (living out), and lady's maid (living out) as well as a part-time yardman, maid, and laundress (all living out). Oral history indicates that employees who lived out were required, on occasion, to stay overnight.[70]

Typically, there were two to four domestics in residence at Maymont. Married or single, male or female, young or old, many household workers resided with their employers—or, in the parlance of Gilded Age Richmond, "lived on the lot." In addition to wages, the arrangement provided workers free lodging, meals, fuel, and laundry services. Such advantages enabled young, single workers to put their wages toward personal and family expenses or to save for the future.[71]

Nevertheless, residential staff surrendered much personal freedom. Living in often infringed on an employee's circumscribed leisure hours and privacy. Writing in 1894, Helen Moody concisely articulated these disadvantages: "Mrs. Talbot is kindly, and Maria has privileges which are intended to make her very grateful; but the truth is Maria has no liberty. She wears the clothes her mistress prescribes; she sees her friends when and where her mistress allows; she eats, sleeps, and moves always under direction. And she does this for twenty-four hours out of the twenty-four! She may not always be under orders, but she is always under authority."[72]

Every day, on constant call, live-in workers faced duties that were unlimited and indefinite. Breaks came sporadically between chores. Staff toilets and bathrooms were typically in the far reaches of a house or outdoors all together.[73] At Maymont House, a fully equipped servants' bathroom was located at the top of the backstairs on the third floor; a single toilet designated for employee use was located adjoining the coal-storage room in the basement. Late afternoon hours sometimes afforded time for a brief rest before staff members freshened up and changed into evening uniforms. Retiring to their bedrooms about 9 or 10 P.M., they slept with an ear open. A bell could ring in the night, summoning them to dress and hurry upstairs. During time off—one or two evenings a week—they returned to independent residences and reconnected with family, church, and community. Spouses were reunited; parents could spend precious hours with children, who resided with grandparents, aunts, and uncles.

Describing the lot of Maymont's head cook, Frances Twiggs Walker, Hannah Walker Kenney told her granddaughter, "Mother worked hard." As a live-in domestic her entire adult life, Frances Walker could usually visit her children once a week. In the meantime, Hannah Kenney related, other family members cared for them. There was one particularly bleak Christmas when there were no gifts for the children. As the Walker siblings grew older, they helped look out for each other. "Joe and Tom [the oldest brothers] did the best they could," Mrs. Kenney said.[74]

The next generation also relied on extended family for child care when assuming live-in positions. In the early 1920s young Frances Walker—named for her mother—worked at Maymont as second cook. Over the following decades, she continued to work as a live-in cook or maid in white households in Richmond and Philadelphia, necessitating her absence from her three children, Doris, Johnny, and Joseph. "I would only see her on Thursday afternoons, and maybe every other Sunday," recalled Doris Woodson, who boarded as a child in a series of Philadelphia and Richmond households. "So I don't remember a lot about my mother except in those interim periods, when I would see her when she would come home. She'd take me to visit people sometimes. . . . She was a very quiet, a very, very hard working person—truly committed to the job that she had to do for the families that she worked for." Doris Woodson's brother Johnny Walker, retired marine and longtime doorkeeper for the Virginia General

Assembly, had far fewer visits. His mother lived and worked in Philadelphia, while he resided in Richmond with his Aunt Hannah. "I love my mother, but we were split," he noted. "Coming up, we didn't have that togetherness. . . . I can't remember a time we all sat down and ate together. And that's a heavy load to carry."[75]

At times married employees also lived in, returning to their spouses on afternoons and evenings off. Speaking of her childhood nursemaid, Maggie Berry Brown, Mate Converse recalled that Mrs. Brown's husband resided across the James River in Manchester. "He probably saw very little of his wife; she was with us," she observed. For the three to four months over the summer, Maggie Brown also relocated with the Branch family to White Sulphur Springs, West Virginia.[76]

Typically housed in small, sparsely furnished rooms in top floors or basements or in outbuildings of an employer's residence, servants knew that they were to be soundless and invisible members of the household. An ensuing sense of isolation was amplified for sole African American workers, living with a white family and in a white community during a time of strict segregation. In large, multiservant households, however, workers could find support and company within the circle of domestic workers in the surrounding neighborhood. Mary Anderson recalled that "staying on the lot" away from her family was the most difficult part of her job as a live-in nursemaid. When the work was done for the evening, she was sometimes allowed to visit staff members from houses nearby. Often the butlers and cooks were married and had rooms over their employers' garages. Off-duty workers in the neighborhood would congregate there. "Good times, then," she remembered.[77]

Throughout their working years as a butler and cook in Richmond and surrounding counties, Melvin and Hattie Wilkerson typically resided in an upstairs room or an adjacent garage apartment. Despite the constant proximity to their employers, Hattie Wilkerson recalled that they were rarely summoned after 8:30 p.m. "When we went home, we was free," she noted. "After we washed up the dishes after supper, we was free." She emphasized, "We were lucky to get good people. . . . It wasn't like they were slaving us, or anything. They weren't that type of people." The married couple became acquainted with other staff members in houses in the Westhampton neighborhood, alternating visits and occasional card games on their Thursday evenings off. "Yeah, we hung out together. That's how we did it," Melvin Wilkerson remembered. "We used to go out together; we'd have parties sometimes at the house. [Our employers] would leave money for us to have a party." Reflecting on his experiences as a live-in butler, Mr. Wilkerson said, "I just thought that I was at home. . . . You *are* at home, when you're there. That's your home just as well as it is theirs. . . . I respected it as it was mine; I treated it as if it was mine. You want it clean, so you're paying me to clean it, and I'm going to clean. It's that simple."[78]

When domestic employees had a choice, they overwhelmingly preferred to live out. Living away from the employer, which eventually surpassed live-in service after the 1920s, had its origins in the post–Civil War South. Emancipated slaves, with aspirations of autonomy, left the quarters behind the "big house" for separate housing elsewhere. By residing outside the place of employment, they established clearer boundaries between employer and employee, work and leisure hours. "Our maid would not *live in* and was taken back and forth to Westham each day, a settlement west of our home," Clara Backer Epps commented when remembering the staff in her parents' Grove Avenue household in the 1890s-1900s. Noting a similar stance taken by some of the African American employees that served in her childhood home, Maria Hoar recalled, "That was part of their independence. It was important to be themselves."[79]

Like residential staff, live-out employees worked every day of the week, with one or two afternoons off. At the same time they had specific assignments, a set number of hours, and increased autonomy in setting their own pace and approach to chores. They could also find other avenues of income at night, such as sewing or catering. The most-valued advantage of living out, of course, was the employee's ability to return at night to home and family. Balancing long hours on the job with spouses, children, and chores at home was always a challenge, however. "People who didn't stay there at night," Doris Woodson recalled, "would usually leave a little bit earlier. But it was usually dark when they left. You'd see all these people standing on the street corners waiting for the streetcars, later buses, with their bags or packages of leftover food—whatever they'd be taking home to their own families." Nevertheless, Ms. Woodson noted, there was little to no time or energy at the end of the long day:

> Nothing. . . . Wash your collar, cuffs, and little caplet; iron it and get ready for the next morning. Get up, catch the streetcar or bus, and go back. And it took forever, because employers weren't living in the city where you were living. . . . They were living out [in the suburbs]. Sometimes public transportation didn't even run out there. . . . Then they had to walk from the gate to the mansion. Just look how long it is from the gate to Maymont House—that's a nice little walk. Particularly at night, when you're tired.[80]

As was the case for Frances Twiggs Walker and her grown children, their friends, extended family, and neighbors would often provide child care. If a worker's place of employment was close to her own residence, she could find some time in the day to check on her household. On occasion she might bring her children to work—a practice discouraged by most employers, although oral history indicates that Sallie Dooley tolerated the occasional visit of a child or two at Maymont. In some locations in the city, there were other resources. Richmond's Working Woman's Home, founded by black community leader Julia Crawford, operated as a small day-care facility. "At this Home," a 1911 YWCA study noted, "children are left by their mothers while they work, their mothers calling at night, paying 10¢ per day for care of the child."[81]

Beginning in the early twentieth century, many household workers eventually left the employ of a single residence to enter "days work," the piecing together of jobs at different households through the week. This approach to domestic employment had both positive and negative aspects. Audrey Smith observed the working and living arrangements of the Maymont staff—including the live-out status of her mother, Georgia Anderson—and gained experience from her own occasional employment as a day worker. Certainly, she noted, the advantages included the worker's ability to generally choose employers, specific tasks, days and hours. The disadvantages came from the fluid terms of a verbal contract. "Sometime an employer might call and tell you not to come," Mrs. Smith commented, "and you might be counting on that income. Or she may want to switch the day or expand the days because of a social function. Now you might be able to arrange this with your other employer on the day in question, but you may not." Mrs. Smith described the stability, both in income and relationships, which one gained through working in a single household. At the same time, she said, a day worker with fewer commitments gained more flexibility to leave an arrangement that, for whatever reason, didn't suit.[82]

Hours and Days

Whether living in or living out, domestic employees put in long hours on the job. In 1890 Orra Langhorne observed that house servants were expected to work from five or six o'clock in the morning until ten o'clock, or even later, at night. She added that "a great many Southern housekeepers, particularly in the towns, make no arrangements for their servants to sleep under the roof where they labor. Many young girls go to their working places at dawn, and long after dark are wending their way to the house which they call home."[83]

Such extended hours remained the norm after the turn of the century. A Richmond survey of domestic workers in the 1920s noted that 68 percent were on duty more than twelve hours each day and 35 percent worked more than thirteen hours. "Sometimes the employers would tend to try to overwork them, make them do more than what was humanly possible to do in a day's work," noted Doris Woodson. "Servants were already working long hours—overtime, ten to twelve hours a day, which is ridiculous—but that was the nature of the job." Audrey Smith, who visited Maymont as a small child, had distinct memories of bread making in the kitchen—particularly the mouth-watering aroma of yeast rolls as they baked. She also took note of the long work hours of the kitchen staff. Punctuality, she recalled, was the crucial factor in the production of homemade bread. "Everything had to be on time." The cooks had to get up very early in order to get the oven fire ready and make the rolls. "That bread had to be ready. They couldn't say, 'Just a minute.' No ma'am!" As children growing up in elite households, both Mate Converse and Maria Hoar heard the predawn sounds of the cooks making their way to the kitchen. "You could hear her going down the stairs at four A.M. in order to set the bread," Mrs. Hoar recalled.[84]

Following regional custom, Richmond domestics typically received Thursday afternoons and alternating Sunday afternoons off. Holidays such as Christmas and Thanksgiving, key periods of high entertainment for employers, were typically work days for their household employees. Mary Wingfield Scott documented, however, the "pre-Bolshevism" of Willie Daniel, who worked for the Frederic R. Scott family in Richmond from the 1880s to the 1920s. The housekeeper refused to work on Sundays and Christmas, and "we, who had no conception of the Rights of Labor, were made to fetch and carry."[85]

Mary Twiggs, granddaughter of Maymont butler William Dilworth emphasized that her grandfather got up and went in to work every day of his adult life. "To look back on it now," she reflected, "what was really so important that you had to work every day? Meals and household work—that's all." Her brother, Harold Bailey, added, "those people [employers] wanted those services. . . . for people to be at their beck and call. That's what they wanted." If the demands of being in service bothered their grandfather, however, he didn't reveal it to his family. "You'd never know it," Mr. Bailey noted.[86]

Summers Away

The annual summer exodus of upper-class families to the countryside or mountains levied additional requirements on their household employees. Weeks of preparation went into packing clothing and provisions for the season's duration. At the same time the servants undertook extra cleaning and organizing chores necessary for "closing" the city residence. For those workers who departed with the family, the summer relocation brought a change in scenery and, at the same time, a three-to-four-month absence from loved ones at home. For those left behind, the summer brought a cut in both work and pay. Remaining in the city for the season, they drew reduced "board wages."[87]

In his recollections, Maymont estate manager Louis Taliaferro recalled that the Dooleys customarily took six servants with them to Swannanoa: two butlers, two chambermaids, and two cooks. They, in turn, passed down remembrances of the large, white marble mansion perched on a promontory of Afton Mountain. "A castle in the sky" was the way Han-

nah Walker Kenney described Swannanoa to her granddaughter Florence
Archer. Another granddaughter, Frances Jones, confirmed that the "old
heads" spoke glowingly about the palatial residence. Hannah recounted to
her the day-long train trip from Richmond to the Blue Ridge Mountains,
noting that the staff journeyed in a separate passenger car designated for
blacks. Disembarking at the Waynesboro station, they would be met by
the chauffeur and estate manager, who would motor them to Swannanoa.
She described the elegance of the estate and mansion—particularly the
carved swans on the lawn outside, the swans painted on the upstairs bedroom walls, and the large swan bed in Sallie Dooley's bedroom, carved so
intricately that you could make out each feather on the wings. "She told
me Mrs. Dooley had a thing for swans," Mrs. Jones chuckled. Hannah
Kenney also described the extra preparations required when the Dooleys
entertained at Swannanoa. She admitted that she sometimes peeked out
at the houseguests. She recalled that, among the visitors, Lady Nancy
Astor—whose father's country estate was located in nearby Albemarle
County—was particularly nice to the help. "Now there was a lady with
class!" she told her granddaughter.[88]

While away from Richmond, the staff corresponded with family and
friends by mail. As head butler to the Dooleys and other subsequent families, William Dilworth experienced countless summers away from his wife
and family. His grandson, Harold Bailey, recalled the annual leave-taking:
"One time, Papa carried me upstairs and said, 'Now, I'll be away for the
summer. I want you to look out for the family and look out for Mamma.'
When he was gone, he would write every week and send home his check."[89]

Intrastaff Relations

Junior employees in upper-class residences such as Maymont quickly discovered a household's intrastaff dynamics and hierarchy. For instance, the
head butler had authority and expected his requests to be executed
quickly; the lady's maid had up-to-date information about the mood and
plans of the mistress. Having a congenial relationship with the cook might
result in her giving you extra helpings at meals or food to take home.
Moreover, the laundress, though a part-time member of the staff, could
offer important information about other households and the broader com-

munity of workers. Traveling house-to-house, this independent business-woman knew about job openings and the reputations of various employers elsewhere.[90]

Although in theory domestics in large households were hired for specific positions, in practice they often found themselves assuming many roles. The division of labor was sometimes arbitrary in the face of illness, termination, or the simple need to stay on schedule. Staff members helped each other or filled in as needed. In a pinch the cook might wait at the table, or the lady's maid might sweep. Based on stories of the Maymont kitchen that he heard from his mother, Hannah Walker Kenney, and his aunts and uncles, Astor Smith said that the kitchen staff gained some bargaining power with food. As second cook, his aunt Frances had the onerous task of scouring the pots and pans. At times "the basement kitchen was very, very hot—'hotter than Dante's Inferno' she put it—and she had to go outside to rest from it. . . . She sometimes bribed the chauffeur with a couple of the light muffins to help her do the pans. She couldn't give him more than two, because everything was watched over."[91]

Remembering the fluidity of job descriptions among the employees in her childhood home, Maria Hoar said that the downstairs maid would sometimes help the cook or assist the laundress in hanging out the wash. Oral history also tells us that although Georgia Anderson functioned primarily as Sallie Dooley's personal maid, she also assisted the cook and servers. "Everybody helped each other," her daughter, Audrey, recollected. "It was true that they had their differences of opinion. And everybody wanted to make good with the lady of the house . . . but as people, they got along very well." On occasion Georgia Anderson also performed laundry services, taking soiled clothes and linens from Maymont to her own home nearby.[92]

Not all domestic employees willingly took on additional chores. In recalling his years of service as butler to a Richmond family, Melvin Wilkerson related that he was also asked by his employer to keep the automobiles clean. "I told her, 'I'm going to take care of the cars, because I know how they do cars. But you need a little more yeast in the bread. It ain't rising.' She said, 'What do you mean?' I told her, 'You're not paying me enough. That's what I'm trying to tell you.' I got it though."[93]

Wages and Benefits

Wages for household employees varied according to a community's demand for domestics, the household's budget, and the neediness of a worker who might take a job at any price. In Gilded Age Richmond, salaries for the working class were generally meager. In 1888 the U.S. Commissioner of Labor determined that, of twenty-five major cities, Richmond ranked the lowest for weekly wages for laborers—$3.93 a week, compared to the national average of $5.24. By 1890 Richmond's African American workers— 80 percent employed in industry, transportation, and domestic service— struggled to earn $300 a year, far below a living wage.[94] A 1920s survey of black Richmonders placed the average salary of domestic employees, including cooks, maids, drivers, butlers, and laundresses, at $52.00 a month. (The report notes, however, that the figure was inflated by the higher wages of menservants, with butlers averaging $68 and chauffeurs $87 a month.)[95]

The Dooleys paid their household staff wages comparable to if not slightly higher than those tendered in other upper-class residences in Richmond.[96] Many employees came to Maymont with experience and expertise that helped them garner salaries in the higher ranges. There are no extant records of wages from Maymont's earlier decades. A letter from Sallie Dooley's niece, Florence Elder, however, documents a monthly payroll in 1923:

William [Dilworth, butler]	100.00
Justin [Simms, second butler]	60.00
Frances [Walker, head cook]	43.00
Fannie [Waddy, lady's maid]	30.00
Rosa [Jones(?), housemaid]	30.00
Kitchen Maid [unnamed]	20.00
Laundress [unnamed]	15.00

Other household accounts from the same period show that the Dooleys' white chauffeur, C. Hamilton Fitzgerald, received approximately $140 a month ($32.50 a week). Part-time laundress and general maid at Swannanoa Rosa Brown was paid 15¢ an hour. Working a ten- to twenty-hour week for the Dooleys, she made at most $13 a month.[97] (See table 1.) The significant variation in amounts indicates a differing pay scale between white and black, male and female, and skilled and semiskilled employees as well as those living out and living in. Head butlers and cooks typically earned higher wages in compensation for specialized skills as well as supervisory responsibilities.

Maymont wages, while meeting and at times exceeding average salaries for black domestics in Richmond, were nevertheless low when taking into account the typical worker's seventy-two-hour week. Moreover, even the highest of the salaries could not have covered expenditures for clothing, transportation, fuel, and food necessary to maintain a family's comfortable standard of living. A report on the welfare of black Richmonders in the 1920s noted: "household and domestic service in Richmond can not be expected to contribute much toward making Negro home-life normal, happy and safely above the line of dependency."[98]

At the top of his profession in 1923, head butler William Dilworth earned a wage of $100 a month—the highest of Maymont's black employees. Compared to the average monthly income of African American men in Richmond, his pay exceeded that of other butlers ($68), unskilled ironworkers ($76); black teachers in city schools ($91), and tobacco-factory laborers ($78). Skilled ironworkers made slightly more ($109). Compared to wages across the United States, Dilworth's pay ranked just above that of the average unskilled male laborer ($95). (See table 2.) Could William Dilworth support his wife and three children? His annual income of $1,200 fell below the 1920 living wage of $1,400 for a family of five. According to his grandchildren, his wife, Mary Fields Dilworth, supplemented his wages by taking in wash.[99]

Benefits for domestic workers did not include the employee "package" one thinks of today—paid holidays, sick days, health and life insurance, and retirement contributions. Instead, workers customarily received nonwage benefits in the form of meals, lodging, and fuel for live-in workers and occasional assistance with transportation. Depending on the household, its budget, and its customs, staff meals could range from lavish to subsistence level. Mabel Walker, former bookkeeper at A. Eichel & Co. market, recalled James Dooley's regular visits to the meat counter to choose lesser cuts for his employees. She noted, "He didn't buy any meat with a bone in it for the servants. . . . He'd go all over the market seeing what he could buy the cheapest." On the other hand, Audrey Smith—who spent hours in Maymont's kitchen as a small child—did not remember discrepancies between menus above and below stairs. She noted, "We ate anything we wanted to. Sometimes, if there was something special some-

TABLE I. *Maymont employee wage survey, 1923*

Among the documents that testify to the economic circumstances of the Maymont household staff, a sole surviving monthly payroll, dating 1923, and estate reports from Swannanoa during the same year record the wages of individual employees. Domestic servants in upper-class Richmond house-holds—with the exception of laundresses—generally worked every day, 13 hours a day, with Thursday afternoon and every other Sunday afternoon off (averaging 326 days a year, 27 days a month, 6¼ days a week). Each worker's 1923 annual salary is calculated to the right; the far right column adjusts the annual wage to 2002 values.*

EMPLOYEE	HOURLY	DAILY	WEEKLY	MONTHLY	ANNUAL[a]	ANNUAL, 2002 VALUE[b]
C. H. Fitzgerald, chauffeur	.40	5.20	32.50	140.00	1,680.00	17,674.00
William Dilworth, head butler	.28	3.70	23.09	100.00	1,200.00	12,428.00
Justin Simms, second butler	.17	2.22	13.85	60.00	720.00	7,457.00
Frances Walker, head cook	.12	1.59	9.93	43.00	516.00	5,344.00
Kitchen maid (unnamed)	.06	.74	4.61	20.00	240.00	2,486.00
Fannie Waddy, lady's maid	.09	1.11	6.93	30.00	360.00	3,728.00
Rosa (Jones?), housemaid	.09	1.11	6.93	30.00	360.00	3,728.00
Laundress	.22[c]	1.73	3.46[d]	15.00	180.00	1,864.00

* FCE to WCB, 14 July [1923]; GGD to WCB, 24 November 1923, Dooley Papers, VHS.

[a] In 1920 the living wage for a family of five was estimated to be between $1,400 and $1,500 a year. See Ryan, *Living Wage*, 106–7; Denslow, "Ideal and Practical Organization of a Home," 52.

[b] Figures derived from the Cost-of-Living Calculator, American Institute for Economic Research, http://www.aier.org/colcalc.html. The 2002 federal poverty guideline for a family of five is $21,180. "Annual Update of the HHS Poverty Guidelines," *Federal Register* 67, no. 31 (14 February 2002): 6931–33.

[c] Calculated at an 8-hour day.

[d] Calculated at a 2-day work week.

TABLE 2. *Wage comparisons, 1923*

WORKER	HOURLY	DAILY	WEEKLY	MONTHLY	ANNUAL
Worker					
William Dilworth, head butler	.28	3.70	23.09	100.00[a]	1,200.00
Mary Dilworth, laundress (private)		.58	3.46	15.00[b]	180.00
Family total		4.28	26.55	115.00	1,380.00
Wages in the United States[c]					
Public schoolteachers (all)[d]	.81	7.31	36.55[e]	158.00	869.00[f]
Unskilled laborer—male	.40	3.65	21.93[g]	95.00	1,140.00
Manufacturing—male	.58[h]	5.22	31.32	136.00	1,627.00
Manufacturing—female	.39[h]	3.51	21.06	91.00	1,094.00
Wages in Virginia[i]					
Public schoolteachers (all)[j]	.52	4.64	23.20[k]	102.00	743.00[l]
Public schoolteacher—black, city	.46	4.22	21.09	91.00	771.00[m]
Tobacco factory—male, black	.33	3.00	18.00[n]	78.00	936.00
Tobacco factory—male, white	.46	4.16	25.00[n]	108.25	1,299.00
Tobacco factory—female, black	.18	1.66	10.00[n]	43.30	519.60
Tobacco factory—female, white	.33	3.00	18.00[n]	78.00	936.00
Iron & machinery—male, skilled (all)	.47	4.20[o]	25.20	109.10	1,309.20
Iron & machinery—male, unskilled (all)	.32	2.92[n]	17.52	75.86	910.30
Laborer—male, rural[p]	.33	3.00[q]	18.00	78.00	936.00

[a] FCE to WCB, 14 July [1923], GGD to WCB, 24 November 1923, Dooley Papers, VHS; Jeanette Bailey, interview, 19 November 1999.

[b] Estimated from payroll in FCE to WCB, 14 July [1923], an unnamed laundress washing for five families (5 baskets) a week, would average .70 a basket.

[c] Manufacturing wages are calculated to a 9-hour day, 6-day work week; Beney, *Wages, Hours, and Employment*, 48–49.

[d] Aggregate figure, averaging wages of male, female, black, white, urban, and rural teachers.

[e] Calculated to a 5-day work week; Douglas, *Real Wages*, 200.

[f] Calculated to a 5.5-month school year.

[g] Douglas, *Real Wages*, 177.

[h] Beney, *Wages, Hours, and Employment*, 48–49.

[i] Manufacturing and factory wages are calculated to a 9-hour day, 6-day work week; Beney, *Wages, Hours, and Employment*, 48–49.

body wanted, they'd make it. It was the same where I worked [on Monument Avenue]. There was no shortage of food and provisions. There was plenty of meal, milk, butter, and beans. If you wanted something to eat, they were going to feed you."[100]

Leftovers frequently went home with workers at the end of the day. "You would see cooks always with packages when they would go home," recalled Thomas Gordon, whose childhood years in Richmond spanned the 1910s and 1920s. This practice, exercised with and without employer consent, was often viewed by domestics as part of an unspoken contract. The food supplemented poor incomes and helped feed their families. At the same time, unauthorized "pan-toting"—seen as theft by some mistresses—could serve as justification for keeping wages low.[101]

Surviving grocery receipts billed to the Dooley account from various stores, bakeries, and meat stalls reveal a substantial volume of food entering the mansion. At the same time, capacity for storing leftovers, even in the larger iceboxes, was limited. "The cook was at liberty with what was left over to divide among the help," recalled Audrey Smith. Her mother, Georgia Anderson, would bring home a variety of food during her tenure with the Dooleys. Mrs. Smith continued, "That's how we learned how to eat all kinds of things, like pheasant, . . . lamb and veal." Jeanette Bailey, daughter of William Dilworth, traveled to Maymont several days a week to pick up excess buttermilk following the day's churning. After eight o'clock at night, she and her siblings would anxiously anticipate their father's return from his duties as head butler. "He always served the dinner, cleaned up the dishes and things before he left," she recalled. "When we

---

[j] Aggregate figure, averaging wages of male, female, black, white, urban, and rural teachers.

[k] Calculated to a 5-day work week.

[l] Calculated to a 7.3-month school year; Gee and Corson, *Statistical Study of Virginia*, 46.

[m] Calculated to an 8.5-month school year; *Annual Report of the Superintendent of Public Instruction*, 16, 35.

[n] *Report of the Labor Commissioner*, 97.

[o] Ibid., 61.

[p] Calculated to a 9-hour work day, 6-day week.

[q] "The regular price around here [Afton Mountain] for common labor is from 2.50 to 3.00 per day." GGD to WCB, 24 November 1923, Dooley Papers, VHS.

saw our father coming in, we used to holler: 'Here comes Papa with the pan!' He would bring the food that they'd serve to the Dooleys to us at night."[102]

On occasion wages were supplemented with cash bonuses and tips. In remembering his years of service as a butler, Melvin Wilkerson noted that he frequently received cash surreptitiously from dinner guests—a gesture that did not escape the notice of his employer, Francis Pickens Miller. "Some people would sit there and talk at the table," Mr. Wilkerson recalled. "Instead of giving me tips, they would wink their eyes. They put it at the center of the floor under the table. After I'd close the door, he'd come and help me put it in my pocket. The floor was lined with half dollars, silver dollars."[103]

Employers rendered other sorts of favors to domestics as expressions of care and concern and as a substitute for or extension of wages. These included lending money, assisting with outside business transactions, making travel arrangements, and interceding on the worker's behalf with the legal system. Also included was the regular giving of gifts. Receiving new or cast-off articles, useful or otherwise, employees generally took whatever was offered. Gracious acceptance on the part of the worker, like the expression of deference, was the expected response. Florence Archer noted that her grandmother Hannah Kenney treasured some of the furnishings, clothing, and other mementos from former employees. She recalled, in particular, an attractive piece of jewelry embellished with roses. "She said her 'lady' gave it to her," Ms. Archer stated, though she did not recall the identity of the giver.[104]

Walter Bernard Whiting had similar recollections. As a boy, he resided in the home of his grandfather Winston Edmunds—head butler for a dozen of the commonwealth's governors between 1886 and 1933. Mr. Whiting remembered the wide variety of nonmonetary gifts from the Executive Mansion that supported their modest household on Second Street. "I never was hungry, never barefooted, never cold, and so forth," he stated. "If the governor ate dinner, we ate. A governor could only be in office for four years. When the new governor and wife came in, they often threw away and gave away furnishings during redecoration. These things often went to the staff. Therefore, when the governor's mansion changed from spring attire (such as Persian carpets for rattan rugs), we did the same thing."[105]

On occasion long-term employees received a pension from their employers—as did Charles Grant Paige, who served as chauffeur for the Bemiss family in Richmond from 1911 to 1952. When Maggie Brown and her husband sought to purchase a house in the 1920s, her employer, Melville Branch, provided financial and legal assistance. His daughter, Mate Converse, recalled that her parents continued to give her former nursemaid financial aid for bills and medical care—as well as a pension—for the remainder of her life. After her parents died, the grown children took over the commitment. "There was no requirement to do this," Mrs. Converse noted, "it was just voluntary. We never dreamed of her not being cared for."[106]

The remembrance of domestic employees in wills, as was the case for the Dooleys and many of their socioeconomic class in Richmond, provided funds to assist workers during a transition to a new position.[107] Descendants of head butler William Dilworth believe that the $1,000 bequest left him by Sallie Dooley helped toward the purchase of a house on Idlewood Avenue, where he resided for the remainder of his life. An identical bequest to Frances Twiggs Walker likely assisted in her purchasing several wooded acres near her childhood home in Caroline County. While her house no longer stands, her grave site remains there today in an isolated grove of trees.[108]

Solidarity Unrealized

The labor-reform movement of the 1910s-1920s encouraged domestic workers to organize in several cities—including a short-lived union in Richmond. Supported by women's groups such as the YWCA and the League of Women Voters, workers lobbied for employment contracts, child-labor protection, standard wages, an eight-hour day and forty-four-hour week, and the new title of "home-assistant." Delegates to the 1921 Southeastern Federation of Colored Women's Clubs, including Richmond's Maggie L. Walker, drafted a document to be sent to white women's clubs. The resulting pamphlet, titled "Southern Negro Women and Race Cooperation," presented seven reform issues. Topping the list was "Conditions in Domestic Service," which included seeking reasonable working hours, sanitary rooming facilities, and wholesome recreation during leisure hours.[109]

These efforts failed. Local and state organizations dissolved without funding and support. On the national front the Fair Labor Standards Act and the Social Security Act, later passed by Congress in 1935, excluded domestic workers. Various amendments enacted in the 1950s through the 1990s mandated FLSA protection in commercial agencies and Social Security and Medicare for household employees earning above $1,200 a year.[110] Nevertheless, to the present day a large percentage of private household workers do not receive governmental protection and benefits. In 1993 Zoë Baird's failed cabinet nomination focused public attention on the fact that only one in four American households with domestic workers complied with tax laws—resulting in an estimated $70 billion in uncollected revenue.[111]

In the "underground economy" of domestic employment, many employers—avoiding confusing paperwork and increased expenses—neglect to pay Social Security, Medicare, federal unemployment, and federal and state income taxes. At the same time, many workers readily agree to work off the books instead of cutting their already-low wages by withholding taxes. The tacit agreement also protects the estimated one million illegal immigrants in the American domestic labor force. The ultimate result is that the majority of private household employees, most of whom spend their working years at subsistent wages, will have little to no income in old age.[112]

The Twentieth-Century "Cleaning Lady"

After 1920 domestic service shifted dramatically in the United States. Native-born and foreign-born white women left household work for new opportunities in factories, mills, and shops. By the 1940s African American women made up the majority of domestic workers nationwide. Until the 1970s the typical American domestic was black, married, and living out. In the early twenty-first century the largest group of household employees is comprised of immigrants from Southeast Asia, Central and South America, and the Caribbean. With improved household technology, smaller families, and more compact residences, only the most affluent households retained live-in staff after 1940. Middle-class housewives, resuming most housecleaning duties, relied instead on once-a-week help. Day workers, in turn, cleaned for three to five families a week.[113]

In 1920 W. E. B. Du Bois tried to imagine the domestic service of the future. He urged: "Can we not transfer cooking from the home to the scientific laboratory, along with the laundry? Cannot machinery, in the hands of self-respecting and well-paid artisans, do our cleaning? . . . Can we not, black and white, rich and poor, look forward to a world of Service without Servants?"[114]

Today, while private residences continue to hire independent household employees, much of the domestic work of the past is performed by commercial agencies. In addition to ever-improving technology in the home, child-care centers, fast-food restaurants, caterers, laundries, and cleaning companies offer specialized services through small businesses and big corporations alike.

Invisibility

While prescriptive literature touted the household that operated like "well-oiled machinery with invisible wheels," domestic workers understood that they were the soundless, near-invisible, yet invaluable cogs. Harold Bailey reflected on his grandfather William Dilworth and his daily contribution to the households in which he served as butler. "It was so important for him to be there everyday. If he's not there, it doesn't operate. He *was* the machine."[115]

Writer Ralph Ellison best articulated the quandary of the simultaneous presence and absence of blacks in American society, a dichotomy similar to the ambiguous status of household servants in their places of employment. In the poignant opening words of Ellison's novel *Invisible Man*, the protagonist explains: "I am invisible, understand, simply because people refuse to see me. . . . When they approach me they see only my surroundings, themselves, or figments of their imagination."[116]

The granddaughter of William Dilworth recalled the conscious efforts of the lifelong butler to work quietly and unobtrusively. "My grandfather went to work to do a job, but to do it invisibly," Mary Twiggs reflected. "To have control of situations, get the job done, [and respond to] 'come and serve me, but be quiet about it.' But at home he was our 'Papa.' He was not invisible to us. He was the heart of our family, our moral compass."[117]

CONCLUSION

"One of the Family"

$\mathcal{O}$n *January 23, 1899*, the *Richmond Evening Leader* reported the funeral of "'Aunt Mary' Eggleston (colored)," long-time employee of Captain George Watt Taylor of East Grace Street:

"Aunt Mary" was not a servant and was regarded and respected as one of the family. She was nearly seventy years of age. She was born in Amelia County, and when Mrs. Taylor's mother died, "Aunt Mary" took charge of her, and always the strongest attachment existed between them.

Deceased was a member of St. James Methodist Church (white), and was a most devoted member. The funeral will take place at the grave in Hollywood to-morrow afternoon, the remains leaving the residence at 3 o'clock. The male members of the family in which she lived will be the pall-bearers.[1]

The following Saturday, the *Richmond Planet* reprinted the obituary in an article titled, "All One Family." The newspaper's African American editor cited the story as an example of the "bond of union" existing between white and black people that should put to rest pending legislation for segregating public transportation:

These are the kind of southern white folks we have to plead our case in an emergency. Do you suppose these people would listen to "Jim Crow" Car propositions for colored folks? Do you believe they would endorse legislation that would lend to the injury of Aunt Mary's offspring or relatives? ...

The gates of aristocratic Hollywood are thrown wide to this humble servant, a member of the despised race. Where millions of white persons, cannot rest for love or money, "Aunt Mary" will rest until the sounding of the last trump.

Then there will be no more abuse and recriminations, no more condemnations and disputes, no more struggling for the supremacy of the so-called races and classes, but we will all belong to one common family.[2]

This and other arguments ultimately failed to prevent passage of a series of Jim Crow laws enacted in the decade and a half to come.

There is no question that friendship, loyalty, and affection were sometimes formed between black domestics and white employers and their families. As workers moved and labored within the intimate circle of a household, time and shared experience would sometimes appear to dissolve class and color lines. "I have seen children who were the spiritual sons and daughters of their masters," W. E. B. Du Bois conceded, "girls who were friends of their mistresses, and old servants honored and revered. But the Service had been exalted above the Wage."[3]

Julia Buck, nursemaid and governess to the Hofheimer children, remained an intimate of the Norfolk, Virginia, family long after leaving their employment. The older woman entered service so that she could raise college tuition for her children. "I feel so proud of you . . . my true friend and first baby," Mrs. Buck wrote in a twenty-five-year exchange of letters with Elise Wright, her one-time charge. "I love you for all the fine qualities you possess." Mrs. Wright deposited more than ninety of Julia Buck's letters in the collection of the Virginia Historical Society as a tribute to the woman who became her lifelong confidant.[4]

Friendship, alongside the expected working relationship, developed early between Hylah Wright and the family she has served for close to seventy years. Mrs. Wright remembered with pleasure that, when she turned twenty-one during the first months on the job, her employer, Isabel Anderson, surprised her with a birthday cake. Still working part-time for the next generation, Hylah Wright described deep family ties between herself and the Andersons: "If something happened to me, they'd come running."[5] Former butler Melvin Wilkerson had fond remembrances of his employer Francis Pickens Miller. On occasion, when he was serving a meal, Miller "would take it out of my hand and put me in his chair. And he'd go around and sit at the table." Wilkerson continued, "Anytime you have a person come to you and tell you, 'You're just as good as I am'—now that's a statement to make in the South! He'd say, 'now, I ain't talking to hear myself talk.' I said, 'I'll treat you just like you'd treat me.'"[6]

With scant evidence it is impossible to determine that such close bonds existed between the Dooleys and members of the Maymont staff. Sallie Dooley's dedication of *Dem Good Ole Times* to "Old Southern Mammies" does not pay tribute to a particular individual, past or present. If we could ask James and Sallie Dooley, however, about the men and women who served them at Maymont, would they echo the sentiments of Richmonder Maria Bemiss Hoar? After naming each household employee in her childhood home and describing their duties in detail, Mrs. Hoar thoughtfully observed: "They made our graceful way of living possible. That day and age when you needed so many hands and feet—and everything to do so much to make our way of living possible—they did it. And we couldn't have done it without them. I feel very, very beholding."[7]

Sociologist Judith Rollins, as part of her extensive research into the dynamics between household employees and employers, worked as a domestic for ten different families. She also compiled oral histories of veteran workers. One former domestic described an ongoing relationship with an employer as "friendship," commenting: "There was a lot of possession and belonging. But there was love, too, you know?" Judith Rollins's response helps us consider the complicated story of the people of Maymont: "Indeed. Love, economic exploitation, respect and disrespect, mutual dependency, intense self-interest, intimacy without genuine communication, mutual protection—all of these elements were contained in this extraordinarily complex relationship."[8]

In crafting the upstairs-downstairs narrative of Maymont House, one can attempt to balance the perspectives of employers and employees. By intent, this study of separate but parallel views results in near equal parts of text. In fact, however, their realms were anything but balanced or equal. No matter the potential moments of understanding or possible protestations that Georgia, James, Frances, or William was "like one of the family," the power always remained squarely with the employer.

The Dooleys moved within a rarefied circle of privilege garnered through social and political connections—and enormous wealth. Beyond their upper-class status, they were also part of the dominant white culture that expected and mandated racial hierarchy. Eminently products of their place and time, the couple abided by the prevailing tenets of white supremacy and supported them—whether advocating restrictive legislation or writing a novel that celebrates the antebellum slave regime. Generous philanthropists to charity, church, and city even after death, the Dooleys' bequests of millions supported an orphanage for white children, a hospital for white patients, and a library for white patrons.

For their part, the African Americans who served them navigated the imposed confines of class, race, and—for most—gender to earn a livelihood. With limited educational and vocational opportunities, they worked as domestic servants by circumstance rather than preference. At Maymont House, where they entered through the basement door and took their meals in the kitchen, and beyond the estate's boundaries, where they rode in the backseats of streetcars, they encountered continual evidence of their subordinated status.

Certainly, the men and women who worked at Maymont House garnered benefits from employment in such a prominent household—a steady income, occasional gifts, and, for those on the payroll at the end, bequests. Cordial regard or affection from their employers would have been a pleasant bonus, but these were not the primary objectives of their labors. "They came there to work to make some money to take home to their *own* families," commented Doris Woodson, descendant of two generations of Maymont employees. "They weren't caring so much about whether Mrs. Dooley, for instance—or whomever—loved them." Ms. Woodson surmised that if invited by the Dooleys to consider themselves part of the family, her forebears and their coworkers would have understood the implicit limitations of such a statement. "Employees were servants," she noted. "They did what they were told to do, when they were told to do it, and they got paid a small salary to do it." She continued, "You *knew* that when push comes to shove, you had your place, and you stayed in your place. . . . You felt like a *servant*, because that's what you were. That's what you were doing."[9]

By the early 1920s, when Frances Twiggs Walker proposed that her niece, Virgie, should become something other than a cook, possibilities for black advancement were closing or already firmly shut. Throughout the Maymont years, social, political, and economic barriers had been erected and fortified to such an extent that they would hold fast for decades to come. Nevertheless, Mrs. Walker's suggestion of a better world for future generations reveals an abiding hope despite the grim circumstances of the day. "I can understand how my grandmother said that," Doris Woodson reflected. "That's the way black people felt at that time. . . . They wanted their children to be educated . . . and they aspired to something better for the children than they had for themselves." At times, however, the odds that African Americans could break through walls of prejudice and segregation seemed insurmountable. Recalling her own childhood as the daughter of a live-in domestic and her teenage experiences as a household employee, Ms. Woodson recalled: "We sometimes felt that *this* was our life, and this was the way it was going be. Until Rosa Parks came along—and frightened us, probably, a lot, and empowered us a lot as well—through her boldness."[10] With the Civil Rights movement, the racial divide began to crumble in the late 1950s.

Doris Woodson—like hundreds of the descendants of Maymont employees—seized new opportunities. She became the first African American to earn a Master of Fine Arts degree from Virginia Commonwealth University. After a thirty-year career teaching art at the university level and now retired with honors as Professor Emeritus from Virginia State University, Ms. Woodson looked at the intervening years with wonder. "My grandmother was a slave. Then she was a step beyond slavery, working for Mrs. Dooley. I'm sure that she would be very much amazed to see what the world is like today, as opposed to when she came along. It would be nice to be able to talk to those ancestors, wouldn't it?" At the same time, Ms. Woodson cautioned, "There is still much work to be done."[11]

Domestic employees at Maymont were more than the sum and substance of their duties. Behind the scenes they were individuals with their own skills, personalities, goals, and challenges. And, after walking out through Maymont's gates, they took with them pride, a work ethic, and modest wages. They went out into the community to raise families, to support businesses and churches, and to help shape the American experience for generations to come.

The following are biographical profiles of known domestic workers associated with James and Sallie Dooley between 1880 and 1925 (including the years before their Maymont residency). These are compiled from several sources: United States census records for 1880, 1900, 1910, and 1920 (1890 federal census records were destroyed); Richmond city directories; Dooley business and personal correspondence, located in the Dooley Papers in the Branch & Company records at the Virginia Historical Society and Maymont House archives; Sallie Dooley's will (codicil drawn June 1923); and oral histories by descendants and friends. Federal census records—sometimes subject to enumerator error—provide such information as name, gender, race, age, place of birth, place of parents' birth, marital status, and children. The city directories offer name and race (designated by an asterisk or (c) for "colored") and, typically, a cross listing between name and address. It is important to note that spellings of employee names sometimes differ depending on the source; therefore, some names are followed by an "a.k.a." (also known as) reference (as: Waddy, Waddey, Waddie), with nicknames in quotation marks. Birth dates, when unknown, are approximated from ages given in census records or by subtracting eighteen (for eighteen years old) from the first recorded listing, resulting in a "before" date listing.

ALEXANDER, FRANK   *b. 1889, African American*
At the time of the 1910 census, Frank Alexander was working at Maymont as a butler. According to census returns, Mr. Alexander was a twenty-one-year-old unmarried African American man who could read and write. He was born in North Carolina in 1889 and migrated to Richmond at an unknown time. As the census listed him with the household, it is likely that he resided in the mansion.

Georgia Lewis Anderson, ca. 1930s. (Courtesy of her daughter Audrey A. Smith)

ANDERSON, GEORGIA LEWIS (A.K.A. "GEORGIE")

20 September 1892–20 August 1948, African American   Sister to James Patrick Lewis

Georgia V. Lewis Anderson worked as Mrs. Dooley's personal maid in the early 1920s. Never residing at Maymont, Mrs. Anderson and her husband, Benjamin, lived at 2024 Gilbert Street near Maymont's Virginia Avenue entrance. This property belonged to Georgia Anderson's parents, James and Martha Lewis. After her marriage around 1910, Mrs. Anderson and her husband moved in and cared for her widowed mother and younger siblings: Johnny, Annie, William, Keziah, James, Mabel, and Grace. In time Georgia and Benjamin Anderson had a daughter, Audrey, and raised two foster children, Russell Epps and Ruby Britt (later Childs).

Georgia Anderson first appears in the Richmond city directory in 1913 as a laundress. She is listed again in 1920 as a domestic. In the 1920 federal census, she is described as a married black woman who is literate and twenty-nine years old. She is listed as a cook for a private family. Her husband, Benjamin Anderson, is identified as head of the house, age forty-five, and a driver for a bakery.

Mrs. Anderson's descendants recall that she assisted Mrs. Dooley with personal grooming and with bedroom and clothing care. They indicated that she also helped cook and serve at Maymont when required. Her daughter Audrey Smith noted that she would do laundry on occasion as well. In the 1920s Mrs. Anderson's brother James Lewis was also employed at Maymont (see below).

After 1925 Georgia Anderson was employed by the city of Richmond as a guide and housekeeper at Maymont House, continuing in that position through the remainder of her life. According to her foster-daughter, Ruby Childs, Mrs. Anderson's appointment was recommended by Sallie Dooley before her death. While referred to as "Georgie" in the Maymont Hostesses' Day Book maintained in the post-Dooley years, Mrs. Anderson's descendants have indicated her preference for "Georgia." Mrs. Smith noted that her mother, an excellent seamstress, also worked part-time at a shirt factory in Bowling Green, Virginia, catching the viaduct train to and from work.

Before her marriage Mrs. Anderson was a member of Fifth Baptist Church; afterwards she and her husband were members of Sixth Mount Zion Baptist Church. The Andersons moved to 705 South Meadow Street about 1946. Two years later, Mrs. Anderson died and was interred at Woodlawn Cemetery.

BROWN, JAMES   *b. before 1863, African American*
According to the 1881 Richmond city directory, James Brown was an African American man at the James H. Dooley residence at 316 E. Grace Street. His occupation is not indicated. Nothing else is known about Mr. Brown, who is no longer listed with the Dooleys in subsequent years.

BROWN, LUCY   *b. 1845, African American*
Lucy Brown, born in Virginia in 1845, worked as a cook at the boardinghouse in which the Dooleys resided between 1879 and 1880. The census returns describe her as a thirty-five-year-old illiterate black woman. Though she is listed as married, the record does not indicate that her husband resided at the same address. It does, however, document the presence of her two children, described as attending school—including one daughter, Rosa Brown (a later employee?). It is likely that Mrs. Brown was employed by Thomas Peyton, the owner of the boardinghouse at the 1 West Grace Street address. The city directory has listings for Lucy Brown in following years, although it is impossible to know whether this is the same individual.

BROWN, ROSA   *b. before 1903, African American*
Correspondence from G. G. Dalhouse, estate manager at Swannanoa between 1921 and 1925, indicates that Rosa Brown served as a general maid and occasional laundress for the Dooleys while they were at their summer estate. One entry, dated 5 November 1921, reads: "Rosa Brown laundry work was for two weeks washing for Mrs. Dooley and two sheets Pillow case and White Spread for William." In summer 1923 Rosa Brown appears sporadically on the payroll for cleaning house, working fifteen to twenty hours a week at fifteen cents an hour. She was hired again at Swannanoa in summer 1925 at the same rate.

Rosa Brown may be the "Rosa" listed as earning a month's wages of thirty dollars in a 1923 letter from Florence Elder. Moreover, this employee might be the daughter of Lucy Brown (see above), who worked as the cook in the boardinghouse where the Dooleys resided in 1880. The census of that year lists Rosa Brown at fourteen years old. If this were the same individual, she would have been fifty-nine at the time of Mrs. Dooley's death in 1925. On the other hand, that individual could be Rosa *Jones*, mentioned in Mrs. Dooley's will, which was drawn up two years earlier. Searches through marriage records, however, have not indicated that Rosa Brown married a Mr. Jones. Whether Rosa Brown or Rosa Jones, the names are so common that it is very difficult to trace this particular individual with any certainty in census or city-directory listings.

BUTLER, R. OLE (A.K.A. "OLA," "OLLIE," "OLEY")   *b. 1882, Caucasian*
The 1920 census indicates that R. Ole Butler was renting a cottage on the May-mont property. The listing describes Mr. Butler as a thirty-eight-year-old white "laborer." Both he and his wife, Hattie, age twenty-four, are documented as lit-erate and native Virginians. Mrs. Butler's occupation is given as "none." The third member listed in the Butler household was a nephew, fourteen-year-old Ray-mond Leadbetter. Virginia born, the child had attended school within the past year and worked as an errand boy for a wholesale grocery. In the city directory the previous year, "Oley" Butler is listed as a farmer residing at N. 8th Street.

Joseph Carter Sr., ca. 1918–1919. (Courtesy of his son Rev. Joseph A. Carter Jr.)

CARTER, JOSEPH A., SR.   *16 March 1888–15 April 1947, African American*
According to his son, Reverend Joseph A. Carter Jr., Joseph Carter was employed by the Dooleys as a butler in the years before World War I. The senior Mr. Carter later spoke to his family about May-mont and about going with the Dooleys to Swannanoa in the sum-mer. The Richmond city directory lists Joseph Carter as a butler—likely at Maymont—in 1912 and 1913. In 1914 he was working as a clerk for Rufus Holz, an African American grocer. Mr. Carter served in the United States Army around 1917 during World War I, and he was still enlisted in 1919. In 1921 he married Sarah Steward, daugh-ter of Otway M. Steward, former coeditor of the *Virginia Star*. At this time and for some time afterwards, Joseph Carter was employed by a wholesale tobacco company, International Planter's Corporation, in Richmond. Mr. Carter was a member of Fourth Baptist Church; his wife was a member of Leigh Street Methodist Church. Upon his death in 1947, he was interred at Evergreen Cemetery.

CLAIBORNE, JOSEPH   *b. before 1863, African American*
According to the Richmond city directories, Joseph Claiborne was a long-term employee residing in the Dooley household at 212 West Franklin Street between 1885 and 1892. His occupation is listed in 1885 and 1891 as driver. In 1889 he is associated by name and address with another African American worker, Major Claiborne (see below), residing on Jay Street. The two may have been related. It is possible that Joseph Claiborne continued working for the Dooleys after their move to Maymont House in 1893, though there is no documentation of this. In

1893 he is listed as residing on Orange Street. His name does not appear in the city directory for many years, until 1919, when a Joseph Claiborne is listed as a laborer. (If this is the same man, he would have been at least fifty-five years old.) The same year, a Joseph Claiborne Jr. (his son?) appears as a chauffeur at a residence on Old Brook Road.

CLAIBORNE, MAJOR   *b. before 1870, African American*
Major Claiborne appears in the 1889 Richmond city directory as residing at the Dooley home, but he is also listed as residing at 1710 Jay Street with Joseph Claiborne in 1889. It is likely that he is related in some way to Joseph Claiborne (above), who worked as the Dooleys' driver for several years.

DAVENPORT, WILLIAM B.   *b. before 1895, African American*
William Davenport, who is listed in the Richmond city directory as "janitor," was employed by the Dooleys in 1920 to 1921. Receipts indicate that he was delivering towels to the laundry. On 18 October 1920, he was paid two dollars for cleaning two rooms. It is not clear whether Mr. Davenport was rendering these services at Maymont or at James Dooley's office. He first appears in the Richmond city directory in 1915.

DILWORTH, WILLIAM J. (A.K.A. DILSWORTH, DILLWORTH)
   6 May 1876–22 November 1961, African American
William J. Dilworth was employed as the Dooleys' butler in the early 1920s. Federal census returns describe him as a black man who was born in Virginia in 1876 of Virginian parents. He had attended school and was literate. By the time he worked for the Dooleys, he was in his late forties, was married, and had three children.

   Mr. Dilworth first appears in the 1894 Richmond city directory as a butler residing in the Richard G. Pegram residence at 316 West Franklin Street—a block away from the former Dooley residence. He would have been eighteen years old. In 1900 census returns describe him as a twenty-four-year-old unmarried man working as a servant in the home of John Miller on West Avenue. After 1908 William Dilworth was working at an unknown location as a waiter and residing at 1408 West Cary. His daughter, Jeanette Bailey, recalled that he served as head waiter at the Jefferson Hotel when she was a child.

William Dilworth and his wife Mary Fields Dilworth celebrated their fiftieth wedding anniversary in 1956. (Courtesy of his grandson Harold P. Bailey)

In 1910, according to census listings, he and his wife Mary (whom he married in 1906) resided at 1807 Main Street. They shared this house with a white street-car conductor, W. W. Fint, and his wife, Burdy. Both couples rented. At this time the Dilworths had two daughters, Martha Jeanette (b. 1907) and Louise (called "Lucy," b. 1909). The 1915 city directory locates his residence at 1900 Beverly (which was later renamed Idlewood). By 1920 he and his family (including a new son, William, b. 1917) were renting a house at 1410 Jacquelin Street, just over a mile from Maymont's Virginia Avenue entrance. As the census lists his occupation as butler at this time, it is likely that he was working at Maymont.

City directory listings from 1908 on indicate that Mr. Dilworth maintained a residence separate from his employers, living out through the remainder of his career. His descendants recall his walking or riding a bicycle to and from work— including Maymont. Virginia Twiggs Alexander—with whose family staff member Fannie Waddy resided—remembers William Dilworth's having a basement bedroom "back off the kitchen." During the day he consulted with the cook, but he spent little time in the basement; "because of the dumbwaiter it wasn't necessary," noted Virgee Twiggs Payne, niece of cook Frances Walker. A 1921 invoice in the Dooley Papers shows that the Dooleys paid laundress Rosa Brown for washing a pillowcase and spread "for William" during a summer at Swannanoa. Oral histories from descendants indicate that Mr. Dilworth was among the employees who traveled from Richmond to spend June through October with the Dooleys at this Blue Ridge Mountain estate.

A 1923 letter from Florence Elder concerning household accounts indicates that William Dilworth was paid one hundred dollars a month, a high wage on the staff roster, second only to that of the chauffeur. Sallie Dooley bequeathed one thousand dollars to William Dilworth in her will. Shortly after receipt of the bequest in 1925, Mr. Dilworth purchased a house at 1703 Idlewood Avenue, where he resided for the remainder of his life.

From 1926 until 1953, he appears regularly in the city directory—primarily as a butler. (Listings for William Dilworth as domestic and clothes presser are probably for his son of the same name.) His daughter, Jeanette Bailey, indicated that he went to work briefly for James Dooley's sister, Alice, on Franklin Street. He also returned to work for a while as a waiter at the Jefferson Hotel.

Oral history indicates that in the mid-1930s Mr. Dilworth became butler in the household of J. P. Taylor at 2325 Monument Avenue. He remained in employment there until retiring sometime in the mid-1950s. A member of Mt. Vernon Baptist Church on Rosewood Avenue, Mr. Dilworth died on 22 November 1961.

FITZGERALD, CHARLES HAMILTON (A.K.A. C. H., HAMILTON)
17 October 1894–7 April 1952, Caucasian Brother to James Fitzgerald
Charles Hamilton Fitzgerald worked as the Dooleys' chauffeur from 1920 to 1925. According to his nephew, Aubrey H. Fitzgerald, Hamilton (as he was known) was born in Nelson County, Virginia, near Afton Mountain. His older brother, James, had worked for the Dooleys as a chauffeur (see below).

It appears that when he was hired in 1920, Mr. Fitzgerald had previous experience as a chauffeur-mechanic in Waynesboro. No doubt he was recommended by his older brother; a surviving letter indicates that he was also referred to the Dooleys by G. G. Dalhouse, Swannanoa estate manager, who mentioned his previous employment for a Mr. Fishburn about 1910. Hamilton Fitzgerald was added to the Maymont payroll in June 1920, when he was twenty-six years old. A Richmond store invoice for that year shows that he was outfitted by his employers with an "Alp Coat." His initial wage was $32.50 per week. In the fall of 1920, repairs and improvements were made at Maymont to "chauffeur's room on 2nd floor" of the "new garage." In 1921 improvements were also made to the three rooms on the second floor of the barn at Swannanoa for Mr. Fitzgerald and his wife.

Surviving documents indicate that Mr. Fitzgerald and his wife resided both at Maymont and at Swannanoa, depending on the Dooleys' itinerary. A June 1925 payroll shows an additional $7.46 to cover expenses for travels to Richmond. It appears that Mr. Fitzgerald was the driver for the Dooleys, family members, and guests at Swannanoa. Another driver, C. M. Speck, was paid by the trip for "taking servants out."

Mr. Fitzgerald had some purchasing authority on behalf of the Dooleys. Several extant invoices from Richmond auto companies and auto-parts businesses bear his initials or signature, "C. H. Fitzgerald." A slip of paper dated 18 January 1921 shows Mr. Fitzgerald's hand-written tabulation of the Dooleys' city and state auto license fees for that year. Hamilton Fitzgerald was bequeathed one thousand dollars in Sallie Dooley's will.

His nephew, Aubrey, stated that "Uncle Ham" was married twice but had no children. After Mrs. Dooley's death and through the 1930s, Mr. Fitzgerald relocated to Albemarle County, where he managed Copeley Farm—a large dairy farm owned by the Massie family near The University of Virginia. At the time

C. Hamilton Fitzgerald, 1949. (Courtesy of his nephew Aubrey H. Fitzgerald)

he was with his first wife, from whom he was eventually divorced. During those years he became interested in the horse business. With a second wife, Julia Cheney, Mr. Fitzgerald relocated to Hagerstown, Maryland, where he began a long career training racehorses. At his death in 1952, he was recognized as one of the region's best trainers. His obituary states that Hamilton Fitzgerald "spent his life training and breeding thorough-bred horses." He is interred in Rose Hill Cemetery, Hagerstown, Maryland.

FITZGERALD, JAMES ROBERT LANE   *15 February 1892–1 December 1967,*
   Caucasian   Brother to C. Hamilton Fitzgerald
James R. L. Fitzgerald Sr. worked as the Dooleys' chauffeur-mechanic between 1914 and 1917. According to his son, James R. L. Fitzgerald Jr., he was born in Nelson County, Virginia, near Afton Mountain. His younger brother, C. Hamilton, also worked for the Dooleys in the same position in the early 1920s (see above).

James R. L. Fitzgerald in full chauffeur's regalia, ca. 1916. (Maymont Foundation; gift of his wife, Mrs. Aurelia Fitzgerald)

In a 1976 interview Mr. Fitzgerald's wife, Aurelia Davis Fitzgerald, also confirmed the approximate dates of his employment at Maymont. Although the two married in 1918 after her husband left the Dooleys' employment, she was able to relate some of his duties and certain recollections of his Maymont years. Young James Fitzgerald had been working in a Waynesboro garage before he was employed by James Dooley. Presumably the Dooleys met him during their summer residency at nearby Swannanoa. Aside from his capacity as driver, full responsibility was given Mr. Fitzgerald for the care and maintenance of the motorcars. When Mr. Fitzgerald began working at Maymont, he lived for a short while in the gatehouse with the family of estate manager Louis Taliaferro. He soon found lodgings with the Albert Davis family in Riverview near the estate. It was there that he met the daughter of the house—and his future wife, Aurelia.

His job brought him to Maymont House in the early morning, and he left in the evening unless his services were required. During Mr. Fitzgerald's employment at least two cars were kept on the estate: a limousine for the Dooleys and a Ford for errands to be run by the staff. Mrs. Fitzgerald recalled that James Dooley would request that her husband drive as fast as the law would permit. Mr. Fitzgerald's employment at Maymont ended when he enlisted in the United States Army during World War I. He served in Army Transport in France.

On his return to Richmond he married Aurelia Davis, a schoolteacher. The couple eventually had six children: James Jr., Beverly ("B. C."), Kathleen (later Bracken), Cary, Gordon, and David. The 1924 and 1926 city directories indicate that the Fitzgerald family resided at streetcar stop 44½ Lakeside Avenue. James Fitzgerald Jr. related that in 1934 his father built his own house at 5324 Bloomingdale Avene, where he and Mrs. Fitzgerald resided the remainder of their lives. In the years following his employment at Maymont, Mr. Fitzgerald worked as a chauffeur-mechanic for Eugene C. Massie at 1835 Monument Ave., as a steamfitter at Camp Pearey during World War II, and as a fireman-hostler for the RF&P Railroad. After his retirement he operated a lawn-mower repair shop until his death in 1967 at age seventy-five. His son, James, noted: "He was a good father, sober, hardworking (worked all during the depression) and raised with my mother a very good family." He is interred at Emmanuel Episcopal Church, Brook Hill Cemetery.

GLASER, GENEVIEVE   *b. ca. 1886, African American*
According to the 1910 census, Genevieve Glaser was working at Maymont as a maid. The returns describe her as a literate twenty-four-year-old unmarried black woman from Indiana. It is assumed that at the time she was living in the mansion. She does not appear on any Richmond city directory listings during this period.

HARRISON, EMMA S.   *b. ca. 1862, African American*
The 1910 census lists Emma S. Harrison as the housekeeper at Maymont—the only time that this job title appears in extant records. Presumably Mrs. Harrison was living in the mansion at the time. The census returns describe her as a forty-eight-year-old literate black woman who was born in Virginia. The records indicate that she was married and had given birth to four children, only one of whom was then living. Neither her husband nor the child (who was probably an adult) resided at Maymont. Mrs. Harrison was employed at Maymont between 1910 and 1915. She first appears in the Richmond city directory in 1898, residing at 318 N. 3rd Street. In 1899 she is again at the same address, the residence of Mary E. Harrison, who is likely a relative. Eleven years later, Mrs. Harrison is located at Maymont as "housekeeper" in the federal census. In 1911 Mrs. Harrison received a postcard (picturing the Corcoran Art Gallery) from a friend who was visiting Washington, D.C. The card, located in the Maymont House archives, is addressed: "Mrs. Emma Harrison/Richmond VA/Box 1840/To

Major Dooley." She continued as an employee of Maymont over the following four years, listed variously as housekeeper, domestic, and maid. By 1920 she is a domestic in the residence of Conrad F. Sauer on West Grace Street. Between 1921 and 1926 Mrs. Harrison was a cook at 1804 Hamilton Avenue, the residence of A. Reid Venable.

JOHNSON, ALICE (JOHNSON LEWIS)   *April 1879–18 October 1938,*
    African American   Daughter of Nannie Johnson
According to her grandson Eugene Jones and granddaughter Amy Harris, Alice Johnson worked for the Dooleys at Maymont House. She likely served in the position of second cook under the supervision of her mother, Nannie Johnson (see below), between 1915 and 1919. About 1895 Alice married Washington Lewis, with whom she had three children: Lelia, Inez, and Charles. With her second husband, General Johnson, whom she married around 1911, she had three more children: Maria, Nannie, and John. The 1920 census records describe her as a forty-one-year-old literate black woman who earned wages in her home as a laundress. The Johnson family resided at 1322 Claiborne Street in the Randolph neighborhood near Maymont. Mrs. Johnson died in 1938 at age fifty-nine and was interred at Evergreen Cemetery.

JOHNSON, NANNIE JOHNSTON   *b. before 1862, African American*   Mother
    of Alice Johnson
According to her great-grandson Eugene Jones and her great-granddaughter Amy Harris, Nannie J. Johnson worked as a cook for the Dooleys at Maymont House. Family tradition also indicates that her daughter Alice Johnson (see above) worked at Maymont—probably as second cook—during the same period. The years of their employment are estimated to be between 1915 and 1919. Nannie, whose maiden name was Johnston, married William Johnson sometime in the mid-1870s.

JONES, FLEMING (A.K.A. FLEMMING)   *b. before 1867, African American*
The 1885–86 city directory locates Fleming Jones in the Dooleys' West Franklin Street residence as a butler. He does not appear in directory listings in subsequent years.

JONES, ROSA   *b. before 1905, African American*
Rosa Jones was employed at Maymont at the time Mrs. Dooley drew up a codicil to her will in 1923. It appears that she was there two years later to receive the

bequest of one thousand dollars. The name "Rosa" appears on the 1923 payroll letter from Florence Elder. At the time she was paid thirty dollars a month. This, however, might possibly be Rosa *Brown* (see above), who also appears on the Swannanoa payroll during 1923. It could be the same woman with a married name, indicated by the middle initial "B." in the 1921 and 1922 city directories. Nevertheless, a search through county records failed to locate a Rosa Brown–Mr. Jones marriage. As hers is such a common name, it is very difficult to trace a particular Rosa Jones with any certainty through the city directories or other public records.

LACKMIOK, EMILY (A.K.A. LACKMICK)   *b. February 1874, Caucasian*
The 1900 federal census lists Emily Lackmiok as one of two servants residing in the Dooley household at Maymont. Returns describe Miss Lackmiok as a twenty-six-year-old white woman who was born in Germany to a German father and a French mother. She emigrated to the United States in 1894. She was literate and had been unemployed for two months of the previous year. Her particular job description at Maymont is not specified; she is listed simply as a "servant." Miss Lackmiock does not appear in subsequent census or city-directory records.

LEWIS, JAMES PATRICK   *21 December 1893–February 1969, African American*
Brother to Georgia Anderson
James Patrick Lewis, brother of Maymont employee Georgia Lewis Anderson (see above), is listed on the 1920 census as a twenty-four-year-old literate unmarried black male, working as a butler in a private residence. His name appears as "James Anderson" at 2024 Gilbert Street—an enumerator error, likely made because James Lewis was residing in the house of his sister and brother-in-law, Benjamin Anderson. Oral-history information from Audrey Smith, daughter of Georgia Anderson, indicates that James Lewis worked at Maymont as a yardman and occasional butler. Virginia Twiggs Alexander, with whose family staff member Fannie Waddy resided, further indicated that Lewis also served as chauffeur when needed.

James Patrick Lewis, ca. 1930s. (Courtesy of his niece Audrey A. Smith)

James Lewis's foster niece, Ruby Childs, has a clear memory of "Uncle Jimmy." After his tenure at Maymont, he worked for Dr. and Mrs. Robert Bryan on Monument Avenue from some time in the 1920s until after World War II. Although he was primarily the chauffeur and butler, Mrs. Childs recalls that he also made a garden for the Bryans and taught his niece about gardening. She recalls, "He gave us a love of nature." Following Dr. Bryan's death, Mr. Lewis went with Mrs. Bryan when she relocated to the Prestwould Apartments on Franklin Street.

According to his niece, Audrey Smith, Mr. Lewis married late in life. His wife was Idelia Haskins, who lived in as a maid for a family in Byrd Park Court. After his death, Mr. Lewis was interred at Woodlawn Cemetery.

LYLE, LUCY   *b. 1840, African American*
Lucy Lyle worked as a servant in the boardinghouse in which the Dooleys resided at the time of the 1880 census. The returns describe her as a forty-year-old black woman who was married and illiterate. It is likely that Mrs. Lyle was employed by Thomas Peyton, the owner of the boardinghouse at 1 West Grace Street.

MORRIS, M. C.   *b. before 1864, African American*
In the 1882–1883 Richmond city directory, M. C. Morris is listed as a waiter at the Dooley residence on West Franklin Street. Although he appears at that address, he is also cross listed at a residence on South 1st Street. He does not appear again in subsequent city directories during the Dooley period.

NETHERLAND, MARTHA E. (A.K.A. "MATTIE," NETHERLANDS)   *b. 1871,*
    African American
Martha E. Netherland ("Mattie") first appears in the 1913 city directory as an black woman residing on St. James Street. The following year she is working as a cook and residing in the home of Dr. Woodson Chambers on N. 25th Street. The city directories list her as a domestic and maid at Maymont between 1919 and 1921. The 1920 federal census describes her as an unmarried forty-nine-year-old "mulatto" woman. Miss Netherland and her parents were Virginia natives, and she was literate. It appears that she resided at Maymont House and, during summer months, relocated to Swannanoa with the Dooleys. A letter from Miss Netherland to William Bentley in July 1921 asks the Dooleys' business secretary to forward her newspaper to Waynesboro. Oral history indicates that she may have remained as a Maymont employee until 1924. By 1925, however, she had begun to work and reside in the home of Martha Bolling on Grove Avenue.

While her last name, Netherland, sometimes appears in city listings with an "s," the letter in her own hand confirms the proper spelling without. Care should be taken not to confuse her with another Martha Netherland, widow of J. A., who appears in the Richmond city directory from the 1890s through 1904. That individual was white.

Simms, Justin (a.k.a. Justian, Sims)   *1887–after 1947, African American*
According to his niece Maude Braxton, Justin Simms was born in Waynesboro, where the Dooleys met him. He married Margaret ("Maggie") Bailey in Richmond. She was a schoolteacher in both Waynesboro and Richmond. Mr. Simms first appears in the city directory in 1918 as a laborer residing at 809 N. 4th Street. The following year William Braxton—likely his brother-in-law—is also listed at the same residence.

The 1920 census describes Justin Simms as a thirty-three-year-old male who could read and write. He and his parents were Virginia born. At the time he was working as a laborer in a coal mine; his wife, Maggie, is listed as a twenty-nine-year-old teacher. The couple was boarding in the home of William and Maude Braxton. Mrs. Simms is listed as sister-in-law to William, which indicates that she is Maude Braxton's sister. There are no children listed for Justin and Maggie.

By 1923 Justin Simms was earning sixty dollars a month at Maymont. Correspondence during the early 1920s from Florence Elder indicates that Mr. Simms was among the staff members who relocated with the Dooleys to Swannanoa in the summer. Oral history from Mrs. Dooley's niece describes him as a butler at Maymont. At the same time William Dilworth (see above) was serving as head butler at a higher pay rate. Therefore, Justin Simms likely functioned as second butler and waiter. His many years' previous experience as a general laborer suggests that he might also have helped with heavier household chores such as stoking the furnace. Mr. Simms may have also functioned as a valet, helping James Dooley bathe and dress when needed. Sallie Dooley bequeathed him five hundred dollars in her will.

Mr. Simms was married and maintained a residence on N. 4th Street between 1918 and 1928, which coincides with his Maymont employment. It is possible that he stayed overnight at Maymont as needed (much as he relocated to Swannanoa in the summers). His niece recalled that after the Dooleys died, Mr. Simms returned to reside in Waynesboro. Subsequent city directories, however, indicate that in 1925 and 1928 he was employed in Richmond as a waiter. Moreover, oral history from Mrs. Dooley's niece places him as a waiter at the Jefferson Hotel during these years. The 1932 city directory indicates that he changed his residence to N. Harrison Street. Through the 1940s Mr. Simms worked as an orderly at the Pine Camp Tuberculosis Hospital. His final city directory listing appears in 1947, describing him as a laborer. At the time he would have been sixty years old. No subsequent record has been found.

STANAN, ELIZA   *b. 1830, African American*

Eliza Stanan worked as a servant in the boardinghouse where the Dooleys resided at the time of the 1880 census. She was listed as a fifty-year-old black woman, widowed, and a native of Virginia. It is likely that Mrs. Stanan was employed by Thomas Peyton, the owner of the boardinghouse at 1 West Grace Street.

TALIAFERRO, LOUIS WALKER   *29 March 1875–11 February 1943, Caucasian*

Louis Walker Taliaferro (pronounced "Toliver") is the longest known employee of the Dooleys, having been estate manager from 1899 through Mrs. Dooley's death in 1925. James Dooley stipulated in his will that Louis Taliaferro be retained by the city and allowed to occupy the Maymont gatehouse for the remainder of his life. In addition to that provision, Sallie Dooley bequeathed him two thousand dollars. The length of his employment, large bequest, and insurance of lifetime residency indicate the strength of their relationship.

According to his obituary in the *Richmond News Leader* (12 February 1943), Mr. Taliaferro was born in Hanover County on 29 March 1875 into a "prominently related Virginia family." He had been educated in county schools. In Richmond Mr. Taliaferro was a member of the Grove Avenue Baptist Church. He was unmarried when he began working at Maymont at the age of nineteen. It is assumed that by 1894, if not earlier, Taliaferro was living on the estate. Oral history indicates that he may have remained single until he was in his thirties, when he married Minnie Davis. The Taliaferros did not have any children.

According to the estate manager's own memoirs, published in the *Richmond Times-Dispatch* in 1933, Mr. Taliaferro was involved with the planning and maintaining of the estate and grounds. Oftentimes, he was directed in these tasks by Sallie Dooley. He described himself as James Dooley's confidant, quoting the major as saying: "Taliaferro you are one of the finest men I have ever known in my employ and you will always have my protection if you want it." Mr. Taliaferro was supposedly the only nonfamily member who had knowledge of the safe combination and was asked sometimes to retrieve and send along certain jewels for Sallie Dooley when she was away.

WADDY, FANNIE (A.K.A. FANNY, WADDEY, WADDIE)   *1875–ca. 1953–1954, African American*

Fannie Waddy appears in the 1920 federal census as a resident maid at Maymont. The returns describe her as an unmarried literate black woman who was born in Virginia in 1875. City directories and oral histories also place her as a Maymont employee between 1919 and 1925.

Because of various spellings of her name—and because a second Fannie Waddy sometimes appears in the city directories—it is difficult to follow her previous residency and employment history with certainty. Oral history and city-directory listings confirm that between 1908 and 1910 Miss Waddy was employed and resided at 906 Park Avenue, the home of Bishop Robert Atkinson Gibson. The 1910 census locates her in the household of Peter H. Mayo. She appears at three separate addresses between 1913 and 1920. By the time she was employed by the Dooleys, she was in her mid-forties and renting a room in the residence of Mr. and Mrs. Robert Fife and their daughter, Virginia. According to Virginia Fife Twiggs Alexander, Fannie Waddy served as a personal maid to Sallie Dooley, helping her dress and caring for her clothes. At times, when she worked late in the evenings, she spent the night in the Dooley basement. Audrey Smith, daughter of lady's maid Georgia Anderson, recalls that Miss Waddy performed laundry tasks at Maymont.

Fannie Waddy was one of the seven employees left a bequest in Mrs. Dooley's will. She received one thousand dollars. Florence Elder's payroll letter of 1923 indicates that she received a monthly wage of thirty dollars. According to the Hostesses' Day Book kept by city employees at Maymont following Mrs. Dooley's death, Miss Waddy was involved in destroying personal papers. An entry dated 26 February 1926 notes: "All papers, plans at the home Maymont (now "Dooley Museum") were burnt by the maid, Fannie Waddy by the order of Mrs. Dooley's nieces, Miss Florence G. [sic] Elder & Misses Glen & Elizabeth Atkinson."

Miss Waddy appears in the Richmond city directory as a cook in later years. A 1930 listing locates "Fannie Waddey" as a cook at 1005 Grove Ave., the home of Martha Bolling. The job likely came through networking; this was the workplace, as well, of Martha Netherland, a former maid at Maymont during Miss Waddy's tenure. According to Bobby Twiggs, in whose home Miss Waddy resided during her evenings off duty, she worked in her later years as a cook for the Craigie family in the west end. Miss Waddy was a member of Second Baptist Church. Around 1944, she became ill and moved to Staunton to reside with her sister. She died sometime between 1953 and 1954. She would have been seventy-eight or seventy-nine years old.

Abraham Lincoln Walker, 1922. (Courtesy of his grand-daughter Vera M. Pleasants)

WALKER, ABRAHAM LINCOLN   *after 1890–1964, African American and Native American*   Son of Frances Twiggs Walker

According to his great-niece Frances Jones, Abraham Walker was employed as a chauffeur by the Dooleys sometime in the 1920s. He is the youngest son of Frances Twiggs Walker, head cook at Maymont in the same years. Family tradition indicates that the Twiggs-Walker family had partial Native American (Mattaponi) ancestry.

City directory records indicate that Mr. Walker had a long career as a chauffeur in Richmond during the early decades of the twentieth century. Like his older brother, John Thomas Walker (see below), he served in the United States Army during World War I. Following other Walker siblings, he eventually relocated to Philadelphia in the late 1920s. According to his niece, Ethel Pulido, Abraham Walker married a woman from Richmond named Emma, who died before his relocation to Philadelphia. He had a daughter, Doris, and a son, Alvin; the latter was subsequently adopted by Andrew and Rena Jackson of Ashland, Virginia. Mrs. Pulido also has some recollection of her "Uncle Abe's" residing for a period of time in New York City. Both she and her cousin Doris Woodson recall that he had some artistic talent. Mrs. Woodson remembered one of his paintings, made on a window shade, hanging in her Uncle Thomas's home. His descendants described Abraham Walker as fun loving and a superb storyteller.

Frances Walker, ca. 1930s. (Courtesy of her daughter Doris Walker Woodson)

WALKER, FRANCES   *6 March 1904–November 1981, African American and Native American*   Daughter of Frances Twiggs Walker

Frances Walker is a daughter of the Maymont cook of the same name (see above). Sometime after her mother began her employment at Maymont around 1919, young Frances was recruited to work at the mansion as well. She would have been fifteen to twenty years old during her time at Maymont. It is possible that she shared residential space with her mother above the garage at Maymont or resided in the maids' bedroom in the basement level. While young Frances Walker does not appear in the city directory at the estate, she is named in the codicil to Mrs. Dooley's will in 1923 and received a bequest of one hundred dollars in 1925. A payroll letter from Florence Elder in 1923 lists "kitchen maid," which may have been Miss Walker or one of her sisters, Mary or Hannah, as receiving twenty dollars for her month's wages. In the post-Maymont years, Frances Walker had three children, Doris (Woodson), John W., and Joseph.

According to her children Doris and John, Frances resided in Richmond until 1931, when she relocated to Philadelphia, where her brother Tom and sister Mary had settled earlier. There she worked as a live-in cook, primarily for the Rabinowitz family. Her daughter, Doris Woodson, noted that she placed her children with extended family during their childhood and adolescence. "So I don't remember a lot about my mother except in those interim periods, when I would see her when she would come home," Ms. Woodson recalled. "She'd take me to visit people sometimes. . . She was a very quiet, a very, very hard working person—truly committed to the job that she had to do for the families that she worked for."

Frances Walker returned to reside with her niece Sylvia (Hannah's daughter) in Richmond in the 1970s and, after an extended illness, died in 1981.

WALKER, FRANCES TWIGGS   *25 March 1864–18 March 1928, African American and Native American*

City-directory listings and oral histories locate Frances Twiggs Walker at Maymont as a cook between 1919 and 1925. She may have arrived a year or two earlier. According to her grandson John W. Walker, Frances Twiggs was born in Caroline County, Virginia. She was of both African American and Native American (Mattaponi) heritage. Her niece Sally Woolfolk noted that her first name was Mary, and her great-granddaughter, Frances Jones, recalls that her grandmother, aunts, and uncles often referred to Mrs. Walker as "Grandmother Mary." She was likely named for her mother.

Frances Twiggs married William Herbert Walker (1864–1931) and had eight children. They are, in approximate birth order: Mary (see below), Joseph (see below), William, John Thomas (see below), Maggie (died in childhood), Hannah (see below), Abraham (see above), and Frances (see above). Mrs. Walker first appears in the Richmond city directory in 1903, residing on Ramcat Alley. She also appears as a resident on Catherine Street with her sons Thomas and William. The directory indicates that in subsequent years she was a domestic living on Broad Street and Boyd. Between 1909 and 1916 she was working as a cook and living at various addresses, including the West Franklin Street residence of Samuel W. Travers and the Grace Street home of General William R. Cox and his wife, Catherine—friends of the Dooleys. Her great-granddaughter, Frances Jones, noted that she placed her young children with extended family members while living in with employers.

The oral history of Virginia Alexander indicates that Frances Walker had a basement room near the kitchen in Maymont House, which was furnished with a bed and dresser. Her granddaughter Wilnette Massac also recalled Mrs. Walker's having a room below stairs. On the other hand her niece Virgee Payne recalls that as head cook, Mrs. Walker resided in a four- or five-room apartment above the garage. Work invoices in the Dooley Papers reveal that in September and October 1920, plasterwork, plumbing, and electrical hookups were installed in rooms above the garage. Mrs. Payne remembered spending weekends with her aunt in this apartment. She also noted that her aunt was in her sixties during these years and usually traveled with the Dooleys to Swannanoa. She recalled that her aunt wore a gray uniform with a white band collar. In an undated letter from around 1921–22, Major Dooley writes his business secretary to "Tell Frances our cook that we expect to come home about the 25th of Oct.," which indicates that Mrs. Walker stayed in Richmond at least some of the time that the Dooleys were on Afton Mountain. Her niece remembered that she elected to remain in Richmond one summer.

Oral history from her grandchildren indicates that several of Mrs. Walker's teenage and grown children—Joseph, John Thomas, Mary, Hannah, Frances, and Abraham—also worked for the Dooleys at various times during her tenure at Maymont. A payroll letter from Florence Elder outlining servant wages indicates that in 1923 Mrs. Walker earned forty-three dollars a month. She was among the staff members to receive one thousand dollars in bequest after Mrs. Dooley's death in 1925. According to her niece, Mrs. Walker and her daughter Hannah then took positions at the Stuart home, Brook Hill.

Mrs. Walker's granddaughter Wilnette recalls that her divorced grandmother remarried late in life. Her husband was a Mr. Mitchell (no relation to Hannah's late husband), and they resided in Barton Heights on Northside. Frances Walker Mitchell died in 1928. She is buried in Ruther Glen, Virginia, next to her first husband, Herbert, on forty-eight acres of land she owned—now property of the Indian Nations of Washington.

WALKER, HANNAH (MITCHELL KENNEY)   *8 February 1900–26 January 1976,
African American and Native American*   Daughter of Frances Twiggs Walker Hannah Walker was among the several grown children of Frances Twiggs Walker who worked at Maymont. Her granddaughter Frances Jones recalled that Hannah Walker (later Kenney) worked "on and off" for the Dooleys between 1920 and 1925. She began as an upstairs maid, then served as cook's assistant.

Hannah Walker also told her granddaughter about relocating to Swannanoa with the Dooleys during summer months.

Hannah Walker Kenney was born in rural Caroline County but went to school in Richmond through the fifth grade. She went into live-in domestic service around age thirteen or fourteen before coming to Maymont in her early twenties. She was first married to Frederick Thaddeus Mitchell Sr., by whom she had three children: Sylvia, Thomas, and Frederick Jr. After Mr. Mitchell's death she later married Hodges Kenney. There was another child, James Astor (Smith), raised by her aunt Maggie Smith.

Her cousin Virgee Payne recalled working with "Hannah Mitchell" in the kitchen at Brook Hill in the late 1920s. At the time Hannah was the head cook and Virgee served as second cook. According to granddaughter Frances Jones, Mrs. Kenney eventually worked at the Greyhound Bus terminal in Richmond as a maid. She remained there for over two decades, retiring in the mid-1960s. She was a member of Moore Street Baptist Church. Mrs. Kenney died in Richmond at age seventy-six.

In recalling her grandmother Hannah, Frances Jones said that she was highly disciplined and sometimes strict. "In fact," she commented, "she was the epitome of that saying 'iron fist in a velvet glove.' Nevertheless, I worshipped the ground she walked on. All I wanted to be, when I grew up, was Nana."

Hannah Walker [Kenney], ca. 1930s. (Courtesy of her niece Doris Walker Woodson)

WALKER, JOHN THOMAS ("TOM")   *7 July 1892–6 November 1966,*
African American and Native American   Son of Frances Twiggs Walker
According to his children Sylvester ("Dickie") Walker and Ethel Pulido, John Thomas ("Tom") Walker was employed for a short while by the Dooleys during the late 1910s and early 1920s. It is unclear what staff position he held. His listing in the Richmond city directory in 1910 indicates his work as a waiter; in 1913 he was employed as a chauffeur. As the Dooleys had other chauffeurs on staff at this time (including his brother Joseph), Mr. Walker may have been serving as a butler or second butler.

Thomas Walker is the son of Frances Twiggs Walker, head cook at Maymont. He was born in Richmond and was a member of Moore Street Baptist Church. During World War I, he enlisted in the United States Army and served as a truck driver in the expeditionary forces in France. Sometime in 1920–21, he married the widow Ethel Tyler Johnson of Amelia County and relocated to Philadelphia. There he found employ-

John Thomas Walker, ca. 1930s. (Courtesy of his son Sylvester Walker)

ment as a cook in a country club, as a production worker in a condiments factory, and later as a construction worker.

After establishing himself in Philadelphia, Mr. Walker facilitated the relocation of his extended Virginia family—including siblings Mary, Frances, and Abraham—to that city. Each resided with him until finding work; his sisters Mary and Frances—who worked as live-in cooks—resided at his home during their days off. Frances's daughter, Doris, resided in Thomas Walker's household during her early childhood. Mr. Walker was a member of Greater White Rock Baptist Church in Philadelphia.

With his first wife, Ethel, Mr. Walker fathered five children: John Thomas Jr., Martha Helen, Mary Frances, Ethel, and Sylvester. He also raised one stepson, Frank Johnson, from this marriage and one stepdaughter, Doris Jones Hudson, from his second marriage to the widow Hattie Scott Jones. His great-niece Frances Jones recalled that "Uncle Tom" loved opera and was a gourmet cook. He was also a volunteer fireman in Philadelphia. His son Sylvester remarked: "My father had a very, very strong work ethic. He always impressed upon us the fact that we had to depend upon ourselves, and that it didn't matter what type of work you were doing. If you did a good job, there was satisfaction." In 1966 Mr. Walker died at the age of seventy-four. He is interred in Rolling Green Memorial Park, Philadelphia.

Joseph Walker and his wife, Estelle Walker, ca. 1940s. (Courtesy of their nephew Sylvester Walker)

WALKER, JOSEPH J.   *after 1880–1955, African American and Native American*   Son of Frances Twiggs Walker
According to his nephews John W. Walker and Sylvester ("Dickie") Walker, Joseph Walker was employed as a chauffeur by the Dooleys sometime in the 1920s. He is the son of Frances Twiggs Walker, head cook at Maymont in the same years. City-directory records indicate that Mr. Walker had a long career as a chauffeur in Richmond during the early decades of the twentieth century. His wife was named Estelle. Mr. Walker's great-niece Frances Jones remembered him as a reserved man who was "always dressed in a suit and tie."

WALKER, MARY   *ca. 1895–1900–1945, African American and Native American*   Daughter of Frances Twiggs Walker
According to her niece Ethel Walker Pulido, Mary Walker was employed for a short while by the Dooleys as a cook's assistant in the early 1920s. She is the daughter of Frances Twiggs Walker,

head cook at Maymont in the same years. Mary Walker also became a gourmet cook. Along with her brother, John Thomas (see above), she relocated to Philadelphia in the 1920s, where she worked in elite homes as head cook. Her nephew Sylvester remembers her as cheerful and affectionate. During her time off she would reside in their home (the residence of her brother John Thomas). When there, she would cook family meals. Sylvester Walker recalls her being an excellent—seemingly effortless—cook. Mary Walker had two sons, William and Sylvester ("Bubba").

WEEDON, GEORGIA (A.K.A. "GEORGIE," GEORGIANNA, WEEDEN)   *b. 1859 or 1862, African American*

According to the 1910 census records, Georgia Weedon was the cook at Maymont. She is described as a forty-eight-year-old single literate African American woman. Like her parents, she was born in Illinois. It is assumed that Mrs. Weedon lived on the Maymont estate. City directories indicate that she was still working for the Dooleys in 1914, but after 1916 she is listed as a live-out cook and/or domestic residing at 908 N. 1st Street, the home of her daughter Ella Briggs.

Mrs. Weedon appears again in the 1920 federal census, as "mulatto," widowed, and literate. At the time she was sixty-one years old. She is identified as the mother of Ella Briggs, a divorced thirty-three-year-old woman who is the owner of the home in which she resides. While her occupation is given as "none," the city directory in the same year describes her as a domestic. Three lodgers, a widow and her daughters, are also listed as being in the Briggs home.

There are various discrepancies between the two census listings regarding Mrs. Weedon's age and her marital and working status. The second listing would place her birth year at 1859.

WHITE, FRANK   *b. before 1874, African American*

The 1892 Richmond city directory lists Frank White, an African American man, as a laborer working and living at the Dooley home on W. Franklin Street. No other documents have been found to trace his working history before or after this year.

WINSTON, JOHN   *b. October 1872, African American*

The federal census indicates that John Winston, a twenty-seven-year-old black man, served as Maymont's butler in 1900. He was single and literate. Mr. Winston was born in Virginia in 1872. Presumably he was living on the estate at the time of the census. Ten years later, the next census describes John Winston, "mulatto," as a plasterer. His listed age, thirty-eight, suggests that this is the same individual who previously served as butler for the Dooleys. Further information indicates that he had been married for ten years to Alice, who worked on her own account as a laundress.

It is quite difficult to track Mr. Winston's employment before or after 1900 in city directories because of his common name. Several listings are given, but they may not refer to the same individual.

Introduction

1. Extant letters indicate that the Dooleys referred to their domestic employees as "servants," a term used alongside others throughout this book to refer to waged household laborers. As noted in text to follow, the word's historical usage was subject to debate in nineteenth- and early twentieth-century America.

2. Hostesses' Day Book, 1926–1961, 8A, Maymont House Archives (hereafter cited as MHA).

3. Virgie Payne, interviews, 17 June 1992 and 23 October 1999. Summaries of these and all interviews cited hereafter are located in the Maymont House Files (hereafter cited as MHF).

4. Transcript of testimony of James Henry Dooley in annexation suit, *The City of Richmond* v. *The County of Henrico, S. M. Dooley, and Others, Annexation Records* (1906), vol. 2, 1814. Maymont is indebted to Mary Lynn Bayliss for locating this important document.

5. Over the past two centuries, people of African decent within the United States have used various terminologies to describe themselves. "Afro-American" and "Colored" were in frequent use in the nineteenth century. At the turn of the twentieth century, a new generation committed to race pride believed that "Negro" was more appropriate. During the 1960s, activists preferred "Black" or "Black American." At present, "African American" prevails. Fath Davis Ruffins explores these changing descriptors in "Mythos, Memory, and History: African-

American Preservation Efforts," Ivan Karp et al., eds., *Museums and Communities: The Politics of Public Culture* (Washington, D.C.: Smithsonian Institution Press, 1992), 592–93 n. 1.

6. *Richmond City Directory* (1913), 1231; Kate V. Logan to Sallie May Dooley (hereafter cited as SMD), undated letter, MHA.

7. Copeland and Wayland, "Lovely Garden," *Richmond Times-Dispatch*, 9 July 1933, V-3.

8. Florence C. Elder (hereafter cited as FCE) to William C. Bentley (hereafter cited as WCB), 3 September [1923], Dooley Papers, Branch and Company Records, 1837–1976, Virginia Historical Society (hereafter cited as Dooley Papers, VHS).

9. Phillips, "Maymont House"; Frances Jones, interview; Audrey Smith, interview, 7 December 2001; Copeland and Wayland, "Lovely Garden."

10. Curran, "Dooley Cohort;" Carson, "Maymont Basement Project," 20–24; Katzman, *Seven Days a Week*, 138; Copeland and Wayland, "Lovely Garden." Lucy Maynard Salmon determined that in 1897 the average length of employment for American domestics was a year and a half. See her *Domestic Service*, 109–10. Two decades later, Elizabeth Ross Haynes determined that the length of service among black domestics in the United States showed a dramatic decrease to a modal period of three to six months. Haynes, "Negroes in Domestic Service," 440.

11. "Gilded Age" was coined by Mark Twain (Samuel L. Clemens) and Charles Dudley Warner, who coauthored a novel of this title in 1873. The term was later appropriated to convey the gilded lifestyles, showy expenditures, and excesses of the following three decades. The name still retains some reproachful overtones. Nevertheless—for lack of a better term— "Gilded Age" is employed in this study to refer generally to the period in the United States between 1875 and 1920.

The Dooleys

1. Caravati, *Major Dooley*, 1–2, 7; *Virginia Slave Schedules, 1860*, 041. Thanks to Mary Lynn Bayliss for locating this specific tax record.

2. Dooley, *John Dooley*, 26, 31–32, 56, 72, 82, 148 n. 10.

3. James Dooley refers to the Civil War in these terms in "History and Tradition Favored Richmond Bank," *Richmond Times-Dispatch*, 3 April 1914, 5. Young Dooley inscribed the back flyleaf of his copy of Thomas Morell, *An Abridgment of Ainsworth's Dictionary* (Philadelphia: n.p., n.d.), Maymont House Library (hereafter referred to as MHL). See also Bayliss, "The Dooleys: A View from Their Library," 2.

4. *Twelfth Census of the United States, 1900*, 242, lines 37–40. The designation "capitalist" also appears next to his name on a listing of "Chamber of Commerce Members Who Are Working to Advance Richmond," *News Leader*, 9 December 1910, 21; *Richmond City Directory* (1913), 441; and in the subheading of his obituary, "Major J. H. Dooley Dies in 83rd Year," *Richmond Times-Dispatch*, 17 November 1922, 1.

5. Sallie Dooley was keenly proud of her lineage, which allowed her eligibility in the Daughters of the American Revolution (she was founding regent of the Old Dominion Chapter). She was also a charter member of the Virginia chapter of the Colonial Dames of America, correspondence and records in MHF.

6. Caravati, *Major Dooley*, 14. The Southside generally refers to the tobacco-growing region of central Virginia extending south from Richmond to the North Carolina boundary. An 1871 map of Lunenburg County by Jed Hotchkiss locates the office and/or residence of "Dr. May" at Lewiston near the convergence of several major roads near Lunenburg Court House. The map is reproduced in Bell, *Old Free State*, 201. A great-nephew of Sallie Dooley notes that "The house burned many years ago but the burial ground still exists." Fitzhugh Elder Jr. to Dale Wheary, 25 June 1998, MHF.

7. Steltzner and Cutting, *1850 Census of Lunenburg County*, n.p.

8. Tax listings indicate that Henry May steadily increased the number of slaves in his household, from three slaves in 1837 to twenty-two in 1850. *Auditor of Public Accounts*. To gain a better understanding of the domestic life of Virginia planter families and their enslaved workers, see Stevenson, *Life in Black and White*.

9. "Lunenburg County, Virginia, 1800 Tax List," 225; Fothergill, *Peter Jones and Richard Jones Genealogies*, 284–89; Beeman, *Evolution of the Southern Backcountry*, 236.

10. Beeman, *Evolution of the Southern Backcountry*, 170–71, 225; "Jane Minor," *Richmond Times-Dispatch*, 23 February 1999, D-1; Lebsock, *Free Women of Petersburg*, 171.

11. Beeman, *Evolution of the Southern Backcountry*, 222–28.

12. *Richmond Enquirer* (21 January 1832), quoted in Beeman, *Evolution of the Southern Backcountry*, 223.

13. Caravati, *Major Dooley*, 13–14.

14. Frances Ann Woodson, Oath of Allegiance, witnessed by JHD, 12 October 1865, VHS; Chesson, *Richmond After the War*, 59–60.

15. Chesson, *Richmond After the War*, 72–73, 96–104, 119, 139; Rachleff, *Black Labor in the South*, 16; Brown, "Uncle Ned's Children," 151–52; "House Servants," *Richmond Daily Dispatch*, 27 December 1865, 2, quoted in Brown, "Uncle Ned's Children," 185. Tracey Weis documents a mass exodus of some seven thousand domestic slaves from Richmond households in "Negotiating Freedom," 202, 220–25. See also the eyewitness accounts of Peter Randolph in Duke and Jordan, *Richmond Reader*, 135–38.

16. The Dooleys do not appear in the 1870 Richmond census. In the 1880 census, they are listed as residing in the boardinghouse of Thomas Peyton, along with Peyton's wife, mother-in-law, three children, and five servants. For a discussion of the practice of boarding, see Cowan, *More Work for Mother*, 108.

17. "Finest Residences," *Richmond State*, 31 January 1886, 4. See also Scott, *Old Richmond Neighborhoods*, 154, 156, 175. The house was later transformed into a hospital and retirement home. *Chataigne's City Directory of Richmond* (1885), 161, 267, 567; *Chataigne's City Directory of Richmond* (1893), 920.

18. "American Millionaires," *New York Tribune Monthly*, vol. 4, June 1892, 55. That Dooley achieved millionaire status through earnings and investments made in the 1880s becomes even more significant when one considers that in the South the average wealth per person was $376. See Ginger, *Age of Excess*, 70.

19. For a detailed discussion of the building and furnishing of Maymont House, see Wheary, "Maymont: Gilded Age Estate," 9–14. Judge Thomas C. Gordon Jr., recalling his

childhood in the early twentieth century, noted that wealthy Richmonders were never referred to as "rich" in upper-class circles. Instead, they were described as "comfortably off." Thomas C. Gordon Jr., interview.

20. Wheary, "Maymont: Gilded Age Estate."

21. Dudden, *Serving Women*, 144–45; Sutherland, *Americans and Their Servants*, 30–33; Aslet, *American Country House*, 101–107.

22. Dudden, *Serving Women*, 119.

23. Elizabeth Miller, *In the Kitchen*, 22.

24. Dudden, *Serving Women*, 119–20; Coontz, *Social Origins of Private Life*, 268–69; Rollins, *Between Women*, 52; Audrey Smith, interview, 7 December 2001.

25. Third-floor servants' bathroom and housekeeper's room are identified by name on a work invoice to JHD for painting undertaken by A. Hetzer & Sons, 10 January 1922, Dooley Papers, VHS. Audrey Smith, daughter of Maymont lady's maid, Georgia Anderson, noted that no staff members slept on the third floor. The "housekeeper's room" was likely used for overflow guests or storage. Audrey Smith, interview, 7 December 2001.

26. Welsh, "Microscopical paint and color analysis"; Virginia Alexander, interview.

27. This may have been due to a nationwide financial panic that year, which brought on a severe economic slump over the following three years. However, the Swannanoa kitchen—completed in 1913 when the Dooley fortune was vast and secure—was also constructed with plaster instead of tiled walls.

28. After the introduction of the sewing machine in the early 1850s, factory-made clothing entered the American marketplace. The first ready-to-wear clothing marketed was for men and boys. Cowan, *More Work for Mother*, 74.

29. WPA interviews with former slaves record domestic tasks undertaken by slave women, including the making of clothing for their white owners. See Perdue, Barden, and Phillips, *Weevils in the Wheat*, 96, 226–27. Historian David Katzman contends that southern housewives were less likely to take an active supervisory role in housework and were more dependent upon the advice of their servants on matters of procedure, equipment, and food. Katzman, *Seven Days a Week*, 123–24.

30. See chapter three in Cowan, *More Work for Mother*, 40–68.

31. See chapter four in Cowan, *More Work for Mother*, 69–101; Dudden, *Serving Women*, 124–31. See also the excellent timelines compiled in Nell Du Vall, *Domestic Technology: A Chronology of Developments* (Boston: G. K. Hall, 1988).

32. Worthington, "Report on Inspection of Maymont Household Systems," 1995. Electrical appliances had threaded plugs (much like the end of today's lightbulbs) that screwed into wall sockets or light fixtures. Maymont's kitchen light fixture has two sockets, allowing the cook both to have light and to use an electric appliance at the same time. Most basement rooms, however, had single light fixtures. Adapters, creating dual sockets, came into use after World War I.

33. Several invoices to JHD and SMD from Gregory & Graham Co. and J. H. Chappell & Brothers Co. between May 1920 and December 1923 indicate multiple repairs and rebuilding of the Majestic range, model no. 557, in Maymont's basement. Dooley Papers, VHS.

34. GGD to JHD, 11 February 1920 and 17 July 1920, Dooley Papers, VHS.

35. Maria Hoar, interview, 30 March 1999; Mate Converse, interview, 8 April 1999; Katzman, *Seven Days a Week*, 129–30.

36. Cowan, *More Work for Mother*, 100–101.

37. Sutherland, *Americans and Their Servants*, 12–16; Katzman, *Seven Days a Week*, 282.

38. Veblen, *Theory of the Leisure Class*, 44–45, 62–63, 74–75; Weis, "Negotiating Freedom," 240.

39. Dudden, *Serving Women*, 1; Woloch, *Women and the American Experience*, 295.

40. C. Arnold Anderson and Mary Jean Bowman called the South a "housewife's utopia" because of the vast numbers of available black domestics who would work for low wages. See their "Vanishing Servant and the Contemporary Status System of the American South," 223. Du Bois, "Negroes of Farmville, Virginia," 21; Langhorne, "Domestic Service in the South," 171.

41. Census listings for 1880, 1900, 1920 compiled in Katzman, *Seven Days a Week*, 61; Salmon, *Domestic Service*, 84–85.

42. In Richmond the percentage of female wage earners that were servants declined from 71.7 percent (1880) to 52.8 percent (1900) to 30.6 percent (1920). Katzman, *Seven Days a Week*, Table A-6, 287. Story, "How I Kept House," *Richmond Times-Dispatch*, 8 March 1914, 5; Sutherland, "Modernizing Domestic Service," 242–65; Palmer, *Domesticity and Dirt*, 13; Strasser, *Never Done*, 178.

43. Katzman, *Seven Days a Week*, 118.

44. Ibid., 45–46; Veblen, *Theory of the Leisure Class*, 57; Sutherland, *Americans and Their Servants*, 106–107.

45. Weis, "Negotiating Freedom," 221–22; Brown, "Uncle Ned's Children," 221–23. The percentage of male domestics remained low. The 1920 census figures for Virginia reveal that of 36,925 domestic workers, only 3,144 were male. See table in Haynes, "Negroes in Domestic Service," 388.

46. Dudden, *Serving Women*, 115–16; *Richmond Elite Directory*, 7–9, 23; Gibson, *Gibson Girl*, 62; Green, *Light of the Home*, 144–45.

47. A diary entry on 21 October 1910 by Catherine Cox places Sallie Dooley's "at home" day at Maymont on Friday. Catherine Cabell Claiborne Cox, Claiborne Family Papers, 1803–1954 (bulk 1819–1923), VHS. Thanks to Mary Lynn Bayliss for bringing these diaries to my attention.

48. Green, *Light of the Home*, 144–45; Chase, *Good Form and Social Ethics*, 141–47.

49. "Parade of History," *Richmond News Leader*, 17 August 1977, 35; Mate Converse, interview, 12 November 2001; Sykes, *Nancy: The Life of Lady Astor*, 26; Eda Williams, interview.

50. Maria Hoar, interview, 30 March 1999; Mate Converse, interview, 8 April 1999; Eda Williams, interview.

51. Bowen, "My Friend, Nannie Langhorne," 14.

52. Wheary, "Swannanoa." Routine reports to JHD from Swannanoa manager, G. G. Dalhouse, in the Dooley Papers offer a fascinating glimpse of the life and labors of the estate staff at Swannanoa. Swannanoa's present owner, James F. Dulaney, is currently restoring the mansion and grounds as an inn and conference center.

53. Green, *Light of the Home*, 101–102.

54. Williams, "'Aunt' Charlotte," *Richmond News Leader*, 17 April 1936, 10; Levenstein, *Revolution at the Table*, 15–20; Dudden, *Serving Women*, 122. In her 1885 cookbook, Juliet Corson describes staff duties required in *à la Russe* dining, noting that "this necessitates a greater number [of servants] than any other form." Corson, *Miss Corson's Practical American Cookery*, 119.

55. Henderson, *Practical Cooking and Dinner Giving*, 26–27.

56. Evelyn Easton, a collateral relative on Mrs. Dooley's side, visited Maymont as a child. After a large midday meal, she stated, the butler brought finger bowls. Evelyn Easton to Dale Wheary, 22 July 1979, MHF.

57. Fitzhugh Elder Jr., interview. For the 1898 event, the Dooleys hired New York City caterer Pompeo Maresi [spelled "Moress" in the local paper] to serve a "sumptuous banquet." See "Mrs. Dooley's Reception," *Richmond Times-Dispatch*, 2.

58. Mate Converse, interview, 8 April 1999; Thomas C. Gordon Jr., interview; Cronly, "I Remember It Well," 42; Hylah Wright, interview.

59. Veblen, *Theory of the Leisure Class*, 66.

60. Maria Hoar, interview, 17 July 1999; JHD to WCB, 13 July 192[1], Dooley Papers, VHS.

61. Louis Pasteur first published his germ theory in 1865, which claimed that bacteria caused disease. "Health and Disease," *Dictionary of the History of Ideas*, Philip Wiener, ed., vol. 2 (New York: Charles Scribner's Sons, 1973), 405–406.

62. Wright, *Complete Home*, 125–27.

63. Dolley, *Technology of Bacteria Investigation*, 104.

64. Another manual describes the proper way to bathe from a bowl but adds that "a warm or hot bath should be taken at least once a week to cleanse the body thoroughly." *Home and Health*, 379.

65. Chase, *Good Form and Social Ethics*, 102–105; *Home and Health*, 406.

66. Mate Converse, interview, 12 November 2001.

67. Dudden, *Serving Women*, 139–44; Cowan, *More Work for Mother*, 170–72; Hart, "What a Mother Can Do for Her Daughter," 161–62.

68. Descriptions of Sallie Dooley's gowns appear in the *Richmond Dispatch*, 28 January 1892, 1; *Richmond Dispatch*, 4 February 1892, 1; *Richmond Times-Dispatch*, 10 February 1898, 2; *Richmond News Leader*, 21 February 1906, 7; and *Richmond Times-Dispatch*, 7 December 1912, 5.

69. Veblen, *Theory of the Leisure Class*, 179.

70. Friends and descendants have described Georgia Anderson and Fannie Waddy as personal maids to Mrs. Dooley. Audrey Smith, interview, 27 September 1994; Virginia Alexander, interview.

71. Roseann Tatum Hester to Dale Wheary, 1993.

72. Evelyn H. Chase to WCB, 12 September 1921, Dooley Papers, VHS.

73. Audrey Smith, interviews, 27 September 1994, 7 December 2001; O. H. Berry Co. to JHD, invoice for "Alp Coat—Mr. Fitzgerald, $10.00," 1 July 1920, Dooley Papers, VHS; photo of James R. L. Fitzgerald in his uniform, 1916, MHA.

74. Salmon, *Domestic Service*, 57; Sutherland, *Americans and Their Servants*, 128–29; Turner, *What the Butler Saw*, 181.

75. "Correct Aprons for Maids," 47; McClure and Eberlein, *House Furnishing and Decoration*, 191.

76. Maria Hoar, interview, 30 March 1999; Hylah Wright, interview; Mate Converse, interview, 8 April, 1999.

77. Cited in Dabney, *Virginia*, 260.

78. Winn, "Memories of East Franklin Street," 9. Black domestics sometimes wore head wraps with their uniforms. The custom of wrapping the head originated in West Africa, where headgear not only facilitated the transport of bundles but also conveyed information about the work or status of the wearer. See Eugene Genovese, *Roll, Jordan, Roll: The World the Slaves Made* (New York: Vintage, 1976), 558–59.

79. *Negro in Richmond*, 28.

80. Holt, *Everyman's Encyclopaedia of Etiquette*, 434; Cushing, *Culture and Good Manners*, 235.

81. Rollins, *Between Women*, 124; Litwack, *Trouble in Mind*, 332–34.

82. Copeland and Wayland, "Lovely Garden"; FCE to WCB, 14 July [1923], Dooley Papers, VHS; JHD to WCB, 18 October 192[1], Dooley Papers. Judith Rollins categorizes differentials in address as "linguistic deference." Rollins, *Between Women*, 158.

83. Jeanette Bailey, Mary Twiggs, and Harold Bailey, joint interview, 19 November 1999.

84. Cutchins, *Memories of Old Richmond*, 39. On the eve of the Civil War, Richmonder Samuel Mordecai described "Uncle" and "Aunt" as respectful titles used by children toward older black house slaves, in *Richmond, In By-Gone Days*, 2nd ed. (Richmond: West & Johnston, 1860), 354.

85. Mary Tyler McClenahan, Maymont African-American History Roundtable, 4 November 1994.

86. Salmon, *Domestic Service*, vii, 54–72. The development of the Americanism "help" is described by Catherine E. Beecher and Harriet Beecher Stowe in *American Woman's Home* (New York: J. B. Ford, 1869; reprint, Hartford, Conn.: Stowe-Day Foundation, 1987), 308.

87. Michael Byrne to John Dooley, 11 December 1858, MHA. Thanks to Mary Lynn Bayliss for bringing this letter to my attention.

88. The term faded from common usage again in the late 1930s. For example, in its headings the *Reader's Guide to Period Literature* discontinued the heading "servant" in 1940, thereafter referring readers to search instead under "household employees." The U.S. Census Bureau now uses "private household workers."

89. Katzman, *Seven Days a Week*, 238–40; Salmon, *Domestic Service*, 71–72.

90. Lynes, *Domesticated Americans*, 162–65; Dudden, *Serving Women*, 60–65.

91. Salmon, *Domestic Service*, 146–47, 150, 165.

92. Holt, *Everyman's Encyclopaedia of Etiquette*, 413–14; Trachtenberg, *Incorporation of America*, 72, 84, 157–58.

93. Salmon, *Domestic Service*, 70; Mackay, *Life and Liberty in America*, 46; McCabe, *Joseph Bryan*, xxi; Langhorne, "Domestic Service in the South," 169. In 1898 W. E. B. Du Bois noted the tendency in the South in "making of the term 'Negro' and 'servant' synonymous." Du Bois, *The Negroes of Farmville, Virginia*, 21.

94. "Farm Hands to Get Ginter's Money," *Richmond News Leader*, 9 December 1903, 1;

"Servants to be Paid," *Times-Dispatch,* 9. The legal ramifications of the case are discussed in "Legacies to Servants," *New York Law Journal,* 10 February 1904, 1624.

95. John Dooley, *John Dooley,* 26; JHD to WCB, 18 October 192[1] and 19 October 192[1], Dooley Papers, VHS.

96. Sutherland, *Americans and Their Servants,* 4–5; Salmon, *Domestic Service,* 69–77; Matthews, "Just a Housewife," 32; Campbell, *Household Economics,* 210.

97. Spofford, *Servant Girl Question,* 64–66.

98. Gibson, *My Precious Husband,* 89.

99. Rubinow and Durant, "Depth and Breadth of the Servant Problem," 578.

100. Cushing, *Culture and Good Manners,* 246.

101. Katzman, *Seven Days a Week,* 271; Spofford, *Servant Girl Question,* 159–60.

102. Cushing, *Culture and Good Manners,* 234.

103. "American Negro," *Richmond Times,* 30 March 1900, 4.

104. Weis notes that there were some white domestic workers in postbellum Richmond, but the figure did not rise above 5 percent. Weis, "Negotiating Freedom," 217–18. Jones, *Labor of Love, Labor of Sorrow,* 121–22. Orra Langhorne observed, "In domestic service the white people want Negroes, 'first, last, and all the time.'" Langhorne, *Southern Sketches from Virginia,* 36–37.

105. *Negro in Richmond, Virginia,* 352.

106. Gibson, *My Precious Husband,* 142; Zayde Dotts, interview, 22 March 1995; Curran, "Dooley Cohort Working List," 10–11, 41.

107. Mate Converse, interview, 12 November 2001.

108. Audrey Smith, interview, 7 December 2000.

109. An interesting comparison is the household of Christian Heurich in Washington, D.C. A German immigrant who made a fortune in the brewing business, Heurich employed a large percentage of German immigrants on his household staff. His residence, completed a year after Maymont House in 1894, is maintained as a house museum by the Historical Society of Washington, D.C.

110. Christian, *Richmond: Her Past and Present,* 365; Katzman, *Seven Days a Week,* 200.

111. Becker, *Nancy Lancaster,* 129–30.

112. See chapter five in Katzman, *Seven Days a Week,* 185–222; Langhorne, *Southern Sketches from Virginia,* 36–37; Woodward, *Strange Career of Jim Crow,* 48.

113. Litwack, *Trouble in Mind,* 208–9; Chesnutt, *Marrow of Tradition,* 43.

114. Langhorne, *Southern Sketches from Virginia,* 109.

115. Blair, *Prosperity of the South,* 116.

116. Litwack, *Trouble in Mind,* 119–20; Katzman, *Seven Days a Week,* 193–94; Villard, "Negro and the Domestic Problem," 7.

117. Litwack, *Trouble in Mind,* xiv–xvii.

118. Ayers, *Promise of the New South,* 326–27.

119. Woodward, *Strange Career of Jim Crow,* 70–71; Du Bois, *Black Reconstruction in America,* 30.

120. Dabney, *Virginia,* 434–41; Sherman, "'Last Stand': The Fight for Racial Integrity," 69–92; Meier and Rudwick, "Negro Boycotts," 479–87; Tyler-McGraw, *At the Falls,* 225–27; "Keep the Races Apart," *Richmond Times,* 12 January 1900, 4.

121. Maria Hoar, interview, 30 March 1999.

122. Cashman, *America in the Gilded Age*, 172–73, 191–92; Gossett, *Race*, 170–73, 269–80; Litwack, *Trouble in Mind*, 282–84, 306; Dailey, *Before Jim Crow*, 119–24; Dabney, *Richmond*, 304; Hunter, *To 'Joy My Freedom*, 219–22; "Ku Klux Klan Secret Organization Parade the Streets of Richmond," *Richmond Planet*, 11 December 1920, 1; Ayers, *Promise of the New South*, 155–56. The peak year for lynching in Virginia was 1893, the year that the Dooleys moved into their new mansion at Maymont. Wynes, *Race Relations in Virginia*, 142–43.

123. Litwack, *Trouble in Mind*, 218–19. Thomas Dixon's *Leopard's Spots: A Romance of the White Man's Burden, 1865–1900* (Doubleday, Page & Co., 1902) sold 100,000 copies in its first year of printing. See Gunning, *Race, Rape, and Lynching*, 23–24, 32.

124. Locke, *Negro in Art*, 139; Frederickson, *Black Image in the White Mind*, 323–24; O'Leary, *At Beck and Call*, 155, 182–87.

125. Litwack has a detailed discussion of this phenomenon, *Trouble in Mind*, 185–97. See also Lemons, "Black Stereotypes," 105–106; Clinton, *Tara Revisited*, 196–204.

126. Litwack, *Trouble in Mind*, 215–16; Page, *Negro: The Southerner's Problem*, 203–204, 297; Page, "Lynching of Negroes," 36–37, 45.

127. Terrell, "Lynching from a Negro's Point of View," 856.

128. Dailey, *Before Jim Crow*, 19–21.

129. Chesson, *Richmond After the War*, 106; "Meeting of Irish Citizens," *Richmond Daily Dispatch*, 13 June 1868, 2. Mary Lynn Bayliss first documented James Dooley's membership in the Irish Conservative Party in her "James H. Dooley: Orator and Politician."

130. *Journal of the House of Delegates*, 34; Wynes, *Race Relations in Virginia*, 7; Chesson, *Richmond After the War*, 157; Dailey, *Before Jim Crow*, 36–37. With growing segregationist practices and laws, the number of black delegates steadily declined until 1891, when there were no African Americans in Virginia's General Assembly. Dabney, *Virginia*, 377–78.

131. Dailey, *Before Jim Crow*, 27–29; *Journal of the House of Delegates*, 27, 461–62; *Constitution of Virginia*, Article III, Section I, 8–9; Maddex, *Virginia Conservatives*, 198, 252.

132. "Candidates for Office," *Richmond Daily Dispatch*, 16 October 1877, 2; Dooley, "To Messrs. A. M. Keiley, Joseph R. Anderson, W. W. Crump, and Others," *Richmond Dispatch*, 19 October 1877, 1. Thanks to Mary Lynn Bayliss for locating these sources. She first documented James Dooley's retirement from public office in "James H. Dooley, Legislator."

133. Dailey, *Before Jim Crow*, 1–2; 40–50.

134. Ibid., 142–47, 163–64.

135. "Dooley's Diagnosis," *Richmond Daily Dispatch*, 30 July 1893, 2; "Banquet by the Citizens of Richmond to the Members of the Constitutional Convention," banquet program, MHA; "Major Dooley Pays Fine Tribute to Richmond," *Richmond Times*, 27 June 1902, 3.

136. Dailey, *Before Jim Crow*, 163–64; Wynes, *Race Relations in Virginia*, 51–67.

137. JHD to WCB, 11 August 1921, Dooley Papers, VHS.

138. J. C. Randolph to JHD, 13 October 1920, Dooley Papers, VHS; Thomas L. Dabney to JHD, 11 January 1920 and 4 November 1920, Dooley Papers, VHS.

139. Cited in Caravati, *Major Dooley*, 42.

140. JHD to WCB, 18 October 192[1] and 19 October 192[1], Dooley Papers, VHS.

141. Richmond Taxicab Co. to JHD, 27 September 1920, Dooley Papers, VHS.

142. Copeland and Wayland, "Lovely Garden."

143. Frances Jones, interview.

144. Audrey Smith, interview, 7 December 2001.

145. The average bequest was $400 and the mean was $225. Curran, "Dooley Cohort"; Carson, "Maymont Basement Project," 20–22.

146. Ruby Childs, interview.

147. Mann, *Four Years in The Governor's Mansion*, 320–24; Scott, "712 . . . Hail and Farewell."

148. Maria Hoar, interview, 30 March 1999.

149. Mate Converse, interview, 12 November 2001.

150. Cutchins, *Memories of Old Richmond*, 38.

151. Cleiland Donnan, interview.

152. Mrs. James H. Dooley, *Dem Good Ole Times*, dedication.

153. Ibid., 150.

154. For an alternate narrative to the sentimental plantation story, see Charlotte Hawkins Brown, *"Mammy," An Appeal to the Heart of the South* (Boston: Pilgrim Press, 1919). The African American author, writing from Sedalia, North Carolina, depicts an aged "Mammy" and "Pappy" who are neglected by their former owners.

155. George M. Frederickson coined the term "romantic racialism" in *Black Image in the White Mind*. See also the discussion of the "plantation tradition" in literature in Kaplan, "Nation, Region, and Empire," 240–66.

156. Villard, "Negro and the Domestic Problem," 6.

157. "Review and Magazine Notes," *Richmond Times-Dispatch*, 28 October 1906, E-7; "Book Notes," *Richmond News Leader*, 3 November 1906, 7.

158. Mrs. James H. Dooley, *Dem Good Ole Times*, 5–6.

159. Ibid., 3, 25, 59.

160. Virgie Payne, interviews, 17 June 1992 and 23 October 1999.

THE MAYMONT STAFF

1. The Progressive movement (roughly 1895–1920) kindled reform in politics, industry, banking, the environment, labor, and public health. Nevertheless, scholars have noted that some Progressive reform also supported segregationist policies as a way to achieve social harmony. Litwack, *Trouble in Mind*, 227; Tyler-McGraw, *At the Falls*, 223–24.

2. Mabel Walker, interview.

3. Mary Frances Lambert, interview; Mabel Walker, interview.

4. Eda Williams, interview; Melvin and Hattie Wilkerson, joint interview. The traditional matching of certain chores with days is described in C. W. Taber, *Business of the Household* (Philadelphia: J. B. Lippincott Co., 1918), 263.

5. Litwack, *Trouble in Mind*, 336–39; *Negro in Richmond*, 6. See also Knight, *Negro Housing in Certain Virginia Cities.*

6. Brown, "Uncle Ned's Children," 219–20; Tyler-McGraw, *At the Falls*, 225.

7. Weis, "Negotiating Freedom," 221–24; Hunter, *To 'Joy My Freedom*, 25–26; Brown, "Uncle Ned's Children," 233. The 1920 U.S. census indicates that 85 percent of all female servants in the urban South were black. Of 13,084 black working women in Richmond, 9,055 were in domestic and personal service. Katzman, *Seven Days a Week*, 290; *Negro in Richmond*, 18.

8. The 1900 U.S. census indicates that 25 percent of black married women worked, compared with less than 4 percent of white married women; in 1920, 33 percent of black wives worked, compared to 6.5 percent of white wives. The trend began to move in the opposite direction between 1920 and 1940. See Degler, *At Odds*, 388–91; Coontz, *Social Origins of Private Life*, 316–17; Clarrsia Agee, quoted by Brinson in "'Helping Others to Help Themselves,'" 67.

9. Langhorne, "Domestic Service in the South," 171–72.

10. Interview with Edward Bacon, Federal Writers Project Papers, cited in Hunter, *To 'Joy My Freedom*, 52; E. Azalia Hackley, *Colored Girl Beautiful* (Kansas City, Mo., 1916), quoted in Katzman, *Seven Days a Week*, 84–85.

11. Hunter, *To 'Joy My Freedom*, 28; "Agreement between Mrs. Lucy D. Holladay, and Laura Coleman," Holladay Papers, VHS.

12. African Americans were shut out from the majority of municipal jobs in Richmond during the Maymont era. *Negro in Richmond, Virginia*, 352. Mary Anderson, interview; Du Bois, "Careers Open to Young Negro-Americans," 1901, reprinted in *Pamphlets and Leaflets by W. E. B. Du Bois*, 16; Du Bois, *Philadelphia Negro*, 136–37.

13. Veblen, *Theory of the Leisure Class*, 37; Palmer, *Domesticity and Dirt*, 147. Palmer offers an excellent exploration of class distinctions in chapter 7, "Dirt and Divisions Among Women," 137–51.

14. Doris Woodson, interview, 4 March 2002.

15. Chesnutt, *Marrow of Tradition*, 42.

16. Doris Woodson, interview, 4 March 2002.

17. "Wanted Negro Domestics," *People's Pilot* 1, May 1919, 27, 39. Thanks to Barbara Batson for bringing this article to my attention.

18. Joseph Carter Jr., interview; Mildred M. Carter, interview.

19. Woodson, "Negro Washerwoman," 277.

20. Tyler-McGraw, *At the Falls*, 234; *Richmond Planet*, 27 July 1889, cited in Litwack, *Trouble in Mind*, 145.

21. Litwack, *Trouble in Mind*, 37–39; Rollins, *Between Women*, 168–70; Doris Woodson, interview, 4 March 2002. "Miz Anne" and "Mr. Charlie" were epithets used on occasion in the black community to signify wealthy white employers. Walter Bernard Whiting, interview.

22. Audrey Smith, interview, 7 December 2001; Cleiland Donnan, interview.

23. Du Bois, *Souls of Black Folk*, 202.

24. Dunbar, "We Wear the Mask," 167.

25. Dabney, *Richmond*, 262; Leonard, "How He Knocked Out Sullivan," 4.

26. Katzman, *Seven Days a Week*, 195; *Richmond Planet*, 10 January 1920, 4.

27. Joseph Carter Jr., interview.

28. Jones, *Labor of Love, Labor of Sorrow*, 3, 9; Baldwin, *Fire Next Time*, 114.

29. Hylah Wright, interview; Ruby Childs, interview.

30. Dorothy N. Cowling, Maymont African-American History Roundtable, 25 January 1999.

31. Brown, "Uncle Ned's Children," 347–48; Frances Jones, interview.

32. Maymont African-American History Roundtables, 9 November 1998 and 25 January 1999; Campbell, *Women Wage-Earners*, 239, 243; Pettengill, *Toilers of the Home*, 13.

33. Hylah Wright, interview.

34. Clark-Lewis, *Living In, Living Out*, 104.

35. Joseph Carter Jr., interview.

36. In some cases such linguistic practices were mandated in the South. In 1908, for instance, a North Carolina court fined and jailed a black man for addressing his neighbors with the prefix "Mister," "Missus," or "Miss." As late as the 1930s postal workers in Bolivar County, Mississippi, deleted the title "Mr." from any mail going to black residents. Litwack, *Trouble in Mind*, 332–33. Maya Angelou writes of her frustrations as a young domestic whose employer insisted on replacing her name with "Mary," in *I Know Why the Caged Bird Sings* (New York: Bantham, 1969), 90–93.

37. Brown, "Uncle Ned's Children," 564; Litwack, *Trouble in Mind*, 333; Maymont African-American History Roundtable, 9 November 1998; Audrey Smith, interview, 7 December 2001.

38. Hylah Wright, interview; Clarrsia Agee, interview.

39. Hylah Wright, interview; Clarrsia Agee, interview; Virgie Payne, interview, 17 July 1992. See discussion of the association of uniform color with time of day and task in Clark-Lewis, *Living In, Living Out*, 114–15.

40. James Astor Smith, interview; Audrey Smith, interview, 7 December 2001.

41. Clark-Lewis, *Living In, Living Out*, 160–61. Elizabeth Clark-Lewis and Stanley Nelson coproduced an excellent video on this subject, "Freedom Bags" (1990), available through Filmmaker's Library, New York.

42. Du Bois, *Souls of Black Folk*, 194, 201.

43. Ibid., 193–94.

44. Du Bois, *Negro Church*, 80–83. Elsa Barkley Brown has undertaken a detailed assessment of the development of the African American Richmond church in "Uncle Ned's Children," 28–72.

45. Joseph Carter Jr., interview.

46. Earnest, *Religious Development of the Negro in Virginia*, 151; Jeanette Bailey, interview, 8 January 2000.

47. Jeanette Bailey, Mary Twiggs, and Harold Bailey, joint interview, 19 November 1999.

48. Interview with Mary Tuck, 1974, Mississippi Department of Archives and History and the Yazoo County Library System Oral History Project, Yazoo City Public Library, Yazoo City, Miss., quoted in Litwack, *Trouble in Mind*, 49.

49. Audrey Smith, interview, 7 December 2001.

50. Clark-Lewis, *Living In, Living Out*, 41–47; Ethel Pulido, interview, 12 March 2002; Virgie Payne, interview, 17 June 1992.

51. Salmon, *Domestic Service*, 183, 204–11.

52. Washington, *Up From Slavery*, 219–20.

53. Brown, "Uncle Ned's Children," 77–79; *Thirty-Ninth Annual Report of the Superintendent of the Public Schools, 1908*, 23–24; Richardson, *Development of Negro Education*, 12–16. See also chapter 5, "Education for the Vocation of Housework," in Palmer, *Domesticity and Dirt*, 94–95.

54. *Thirty-Seventh Annual Catalogue of Hampton Institute*, 1905, 40.

55. Hartshorn Memorial College became part of the new Virginia Union College in 1899. *Catalogue of the Officers and Students of Hartshorn Memorial College*, 11; King, *An Afternoon with Hartshorn Memorial College*, 9; Shaw, *What a Woman Ought to Be and to Do*, 77–78.

56. Langhorne, *Southern Sketches from Virginia*, 40; Shaw, *What a Woman Ought to Be and to Do*, 116.

57. *Negro in Richmond*, 32; Emily Brown, quoted by Betsy Brinson, "'Helping Others to Help Themselves,'" 67.

58. Weis, "Negotiating Freedom," 211; Brown, "Uncle Ned's Children," 43. A 1929 survey of domestic workers in Richmond documented sources for job information: sixty-five respondents attained leads through friends, sixty-four from other employees, thirty-five through newspaper ads, fourteen through the Urban League, twelve through the City Employment Bureau, seven through a commercial employment bureau, and three through the YWCA, *Negro in Richmond*, 31.

59. "Women, Labor, and Working Conditions," in "Know Your City Study, 1911." The two agencies mentioned, respectively, are Southern Employment Agency, 211^1/$_2$ N. 6th Street, and Martin & Slaughter, 28 N. 9th Street. Thanks to Gregg Kimball for bringing this study to my attention.

60. Hyla Wright, interview; Hunter, *To 'Joy My Freedom*, 52.

61. Sylvester Walker, interview.

62. Hunter, *To 'Joy My Freedom*, 232–34; see chapter 9 in Woodson, *Century of Negro Migration*, 169.

63. Langhorne, *Southern Sketches from Virginia*, 110.

64. "Proposed Remedy for the Negro Exodus," *Richmond Planet*, 5 May 1917, 1; "Negro Exodus to the North," *Richmond Planet*, 18 April 1917, 1; "Harmful Rush of Negro Workers to the North," *Richmond Planet*, 23 June 1917, 1. Thanks to Eva Brinkley for her assistance in locating these articles.

65. The ad appears weekly in the *Richmond Planet* between 6 January and 17 March 1900.

66. *Richmond Planet*, 29 May 1921, 8. The percentage of Virginia-born blacks to migrate north was 28.8 percent in 1900, 28.9 percent in 1910, 31 percent in 1920, and 36.5 percent in 1930—a high state rate, second only to Kentucky. *Negro in Richmond, Virginia*, 385.

67. Ann Jones, interview, 1 April 2000.

68. Nancy Lancaster, "Richmond, 1903–1913," 37. Thanks to Mary Lynn Bayliss for bringing this essay to my attention.

69. Winn, "Memories of East Franklin Street," 9; Katzman, *Seven Days a Week*, 139–40; Hunter, *To 'Joy My Freedom*, 30.

70. Virginia Alexander, interview.

71. Thanks to Nessa Johnson and Bobby Twiggs for bringing this term to my attention. A sampling of classified ads in Richmond newspapers reveals that the phrase had long-term

currency both in the Richmond work community and among employers. See similar listings, twenty years apart, in the *Times Dispatch*, 18 August 1903, and Richmond *News Leader*, 2 January 1923. For a discussion of live-in service, see Campbell, *Women Wage-Earners*, 238–39.

72. Moody, *Unquiet Sex*, 132–33. See also Brown, "Uncle Ned's Children," 227–28.

73. In his remembrances of Richmond, 1910–20, Benjamin Alsop noted: "Some homes in our neighborhood on Monument Avenue had outside toilets for the domestics." Alsop, "Richmond Recollections," 38.

74. Frances Jones, interview.

75. Doris Woodson, interviews, 13 August 1999 and 4 March 2002; John W. Walker, interview.

76. Mate Converse, interview, 8 April 1999.

77. Dudden, *Serving Women*, 179; Palmer, *Domesticity and Dirt*, 68; Haynes, "Negroes in Domestic Service," 430; Clark-Lewis, *Living In, Living Out*, 122–29; Mary Anderson, interview.

78. Melvin and Hattie Wilkerson, joint interview.

79. Katzman, *Seven Days a Week*, 90–92; Weis, "Negotiating Freedom," 79; Hunter, *To 'Joy My Freedom*, 59; Epps, "2501 Grove Avenue," 37; Maria Hoar, interview, 30 March 1999. See also Knight, *Negro Housing in Certain Virginia Cities*, 115.

80. Doris Woodson, interview, 4 March 2002.

81. Jones, *Labor of Love, Labor of Sorrow*, 122–23. On one of her visits to the mansion as a girl, Virgie Payne heard Sallie Dooley inform her aunt Frances Twiggs Walker that the little girl could visit, but she wasn't allowed to stay the night. Virgie Payne, interview, 17 June 1992. "Colored Work," in "Know Your City Study, 1911." For an excellent study of the residential patterns of African American Richmonders in the Dooley era, see Brown and Kimball, "Mapping the Terrain of Black Richmond."

82. Audrey Smith, interview, 7 December 2001. See also Clark-Lewis, *Living In, Living Out*, 148, 153.

83. Langhorne, *Southern Sketches from Virginia*, 110–11.

84. *Negro in Richmond*, 29; Audrey Smith, interview, 7 December 2001; Doris Woodson, interview, 4 March 2002; Maria Hoar, interview, 30 March 1999; and Mate Converse, interview, 8 April, 1999.

85. Salmon, *Domestic Service*, 134; Maria Hoar, interview, 30 March 1999; Mate Converse, interview, 8 April 1999; Thomas C. Gordon Jr., interview; Dudden, *Serving Women*, 179; Scott, "712 . . . Hail and Farewell," 4–5.

86. Jeanette Bailey, Mary Twiggs, and Harold Bailey, joint interview, 19 November 1999.

87. Thanks to Elise Wright for bringing this term to my attention. For an excellent consideration of summer service by African Americans in the Gilded Age North, see Myra B. Young Armstead, *"Lord, Pleased Don't Take Me in August": African Americans in Newport and Saratoga Springs, 1870–1930* (Urbana: University of Illinois Press, 1999).

88. Copeland and Wayland, "Lovely Garden"; Florence Archer, interview; Frances Jones, interview. The large swan bed and matching furnishings for Sallie Dooley's Swannanoa bedroom are on view today at Maymont House.

89. Virgie Payne, interview, 17 June 1992. The only existing document in a domestic

worker's hand is a note from maid Martha Netherland, written from Swannanoa. She asks that the Dooleys' business manager, W. C. Bentley, forward her newspaper there. Martha Netherland to WCB, 5 July 1921, Dooley Papers, VHS. Jeanette Bailey, Mary Twiggs, and Harold Bailey, joint interview, 19 November 1999.

90. Clark-Lewis, *Living In, Living Out*, 117–22, 140–46.

91. James Astor Smith, interview.

92. Hunter, *To 'Joy My Freedom*, 52; Katzman, *Seven Days a Week*, 118; Maria Hoar, interviews, 30 March 1999 and 17 July 1999; Audrey Smith, interviews, 27 September 1994 and 7 December 2001.

93. Melvin and Hattie Wilkerson, joint interview.

94. An annual income of $1,400 a year for a family of four was determined in 1899 to be "devoted merely to keeping the human mechanism running—cost of food and shelter," in Denslow, "Ideal and Practical Organization of a Home," 52. In 1920 the living wage for a family of five was estimated to be between $1,400 and $1,500 a year in Ryan, *Living Wage*, 106–107.

95. *Negro in Richmond*, 28.

96. Hylah Wright recalled that she made "very good money" at $8 week as a maid in the Anderson home. Thomas Gordon Jr. recalled the cook in his household earning $6 a week in the early 1920s. Maria Bemiss Hoar remembered that her mother, during the same period, drew the ire of a neighbor by raising her cook's wages to $12 a week. The going rate in their fashionable area on Grace Street was $10. Hylah Wright, interview; Thomas C. Gordon Jr., interview; Maria Hoar, interview, 30 March 1999.

97. FCE to WCB, 14 July [1923], GGD to WCB, 24 November 1923, Dooley Papers, VHS.

98. *Negro in Richmond*, 28–29.

99. Ryan, *Living Wage*, 106; Jeanette Bailey, Mary Twiggs, and Harold Bailey, joint interview, 19 November 1999. William Dilworth's annual wage of $1,200 would be equal to $12,428 in 2002, adjusted for inflation. Cost-of-Living Calculator, American Institute for Economic Research, www.aier.org/colcalc.html. The 2002 federal poverty guideline for a family of five is $21,180. "Annual Update of the HHS Poverty Guidelines," *Federal Register* 67, no. 31 (14 February 2002): 6931–33.

100. Mabel Walker, interview; Audrey Smith, interview, 7 December 2001.

101. Hunter, *To 'Joy My Freedom*, 60–61; Jones, *Labor of Love, Labor of Sorrow*, 126; Katzman, *Seven Days a Week*, 198; Thomas C. Gordon Jr., interview. See a contemporary discussion of "toting" in Fleming, "Servant Problem in a Black Belt Village," 8–9.

102. Audrey Smith, interview, 7 December 2001; Jeanette Bailey, Mary Twiggs, and Harold Bailey, joint interview, 19 November 1999.

103. Melvin and Hattie Wilkerson, joint interview.

104. Doris Woodson, interview, 4 March 2002; Florence Archer, interview. For an alternative and more negative assessment of gift giving, see Rollins, *Between Women*, 190–91.

105. Walter Bernard Whiting, interview.

106. Eda Williams, interview; Maria Hoar, interview, 30 March 1999; Mate Converse, interview, 12 November 2001.

107. Barbara Curran, "Dooley Cohort: Process and Results."

108. Jeanette Bailey, Mary Twiggs, and Harold Bailey, joint interview, 19 November 1999; Doris Woodson, interview, 4 March 2002; James Astor Smith, interview.

109. "Southern Negro Women and Race Cooperation." See also Sutherland, "Modernizing Domestic Service," 256–62.

110. Palmer, *Domesticity and Dirt*, 121, 155. For current law and assistance, see "Household Employer's Tax Guide," www.irs.ustreas.gov.

111. "Social Security Domestic Employment Reform Act of 1994," 1–2. The uncollected revenue includes $62.8 billion in taxes on underreported income and $7 billion on unreported income. Greenwald, "Price of Obeying the Law," 34–35; Bauers and Burling, "Nanny works off the books," *Tacoma Morning News Tribune*, 21 February 1993, F-2, F-6.

112. Bauers and Burling, "Nanny works off the books."

113. These demographic and social changes are mapped out in Katzman, *Seven Days a Week*, 271–73; Anderson and Bowman, "Vanishing Servant," 215–30; Palmer, *Domesticity and Dirt*, 66–71; Amott and Matthaei, *Race, Gender, and Work*, 320–25.

114. Du Bois, *Darkwater*, 120–21.

115. Jeanette Bailey, Mary Twiggs, and Harold Bailey, joint interviews, 19 November 1999 and 8 January 2000.

116. Ellison, *Invisible Man*, 3.

117. Jeanette Bailey, Mary Twiggs, and Harold Bailey, joint interview, 19 November 1999 and 8 January 2000.

Conclusion

1. "'Aunt Mary' Dead," *Richmond Evening Leader*, 23 January 1899, 7.

2. "All One Family," *Richmond Planet*, 28 January 1899, 4.

3. Du Bois, *Darkwater*, 116–17.

4. Julia E. Buck to Elise Hofheimer Wright, 31 July 1962, Julia E. Buck Papers.

5. Hylah Wright, interview.

6. Melvin and Hattie Wilkerson, joint interview.

7. Maria Hoar, interview, 30 March 1999.

8. Rollins, *Between Women*, 178.

9. Doris Woodson, interview, 4 March 2002.

10. Brown, "Uncle Ned's Children," 565; Doris Woodson, interview, 4 March 2002. See also Raymond Gavins's assessment of African American Richmond life in the early 1920s in *Perils and Prospects of Southern Black Leadership*, 41–46.

11. Doris Woodson, interview, 4 March 2002.

BIBLIOGRAPHY

INTERVIEWS

Agee, Clarrsia Johnson. Interview by author. 11 October 2000.

Alexander, Virginia Fife Twiggs. Interview by Dale Wheary and Mary Boese. 26 October 1988.

Anderson, Mary Atkins. Interview by author. 1 April 2000.

Archer, Florence. Interview by author. 9 March 2001.

Bailey, Harold. Interview by author. 19 November 1999 and 8 January 2000.

Bailey, Jeanette Dilworth. Interview by author. 19 November 1999 and 8 January 2000.

Carter, Joseph, Jr. Interview by author. 21 October 1999.

Carter, Mildred M. Interview by author. 21 October 1999.

Childs, Ruby. Interview by Lauranett Lee. 8 January 1999.

Converse, Mary "Mate" Branch. Interview by author. 8 April 1999 and 12 November 2001.

Cowling, Dorothy Norris. Interview by author. 10 May 1999.

Donnan, Cleiland. Interview by author. 2 December 2000.

Dotts, Zayde Rennolds. Interview by Dale Wheary and Anne Ferris. 22 March 1995.

Elder, Fitzhugh, Jr. Interview by Dale Wheary. 26 January 1981.

Gordon, Thomas C., Jr. Interview by author. 20 April 1999.

Hoar, Maria Bemiss. Interview by author. 30 March 1999 and 17 July 1999.

Jones, Ann A. Interview by author. 1 April 2000.

Jones, Frances Jiggetts. Interview by author. 12 November 2000.

Lambert, Mary Frances. Interview by author. 9 December 1999.

Payne, Virgie Twiggs. Interview by Dale Wheary and Anne Ferris. 17 June 1992.

———. Interview by author. 23 October 1999.

Pulido, Ethel Walker. Interview by author. 12 March 2002.

Smith, Audrey Anderson. Interview by Martha C. Vick. 27 September 1994.

———. Interview by author. 7 December 2001.

Smith, James Astor. Interview by author. 14 July 2001.

Twiggs, Mary Bailey. Interview by author. 19 November 1999 and 8 January 2000.

Walker, John W. Interview by author. 13 August 1999.

Walker, Mabel. Interview by Judith Clark and Pam Eubanks. 15 May 1980.

Walker, Sylvester. Interview by author. 13 August 1999.

Whiting, Walter Bernard. Interview by author. 2 December 1999.

Wilkerson, Melvin, and Hattie Wilkerson. Interview by author. 10 March 2001.

Williams, Eda Carter. Interview by author. 13 November 2000.

Woodson, Doris Walker. Interview by author. 13 August 1999 and 4 March 2002.

Wright, Hylah Gardner. Interview by author and Mollie Malone. 4 February 1999.

Unpublished Materials

"Agreement between Mrs. Lucy D. Holladay, and Laura Coleman," 1 January 1888. Holladay Family Papers, 1728–1931. VHS.

Auditor of Public Accounts, Personal Property Tax Books, Lunenburg County, 1836–1850. Library of Virginia. Microfilm reel no. 219.

Bayliss, Mary Lynn. "James H. Dooley: Legislator. The End of His Career as an Elected Official." Remarks offered as a "Moment in Time" to Maymont Foundation Board of Directors, 25 February 1999. MHF.

———. "James H. Dooley: Orator and Politician." Remarks for the Annual Wreath Laying Ceremony of the Ancient Order of the Hibernians, 17 March 1994. MHF.

Brinson, Betsy. "'Helping Others to Help Themselves': Social Advocacy and Wage-Earning Women in Richmond, Virginia, 1910–1932." Ph.D. diss., Union Graduate School of the Union for Experimenting Colleges and Universities, 1984.

Brown, Elsa Barkley. "Uncle Ned's Children: Negotiating Community and Freedom in Postemancipation Richmond." Ph.D. diss., Kent State University, 1994.

Buck, Julia E. Papers. VHS.

Carson, Barbara G. "The Maymont Basement Project: Assessment of Research Findings," February 1997. MHF.

The City of Richmond v. *The County of Henrico, S. M. Dooley, and Others.* Annexation Records. Circuit Court, County of Henrico, Virginia, 1906. Vol. 2, 1812–1838.

"Colored Work." In "Know Your City Study, 1911." File 22, YWCA Records. Special Collections, James Branch Cabell Library, Virginia Commonwealth University.

Cowling, Dorothy N. Comments at Maymont African-American History Roundtable. 25 January 1999. MHF.

Cox, Catherine Cabell Claiborne. Claiborne Family Papers. 1803–1954 (bulk 1819-1923). VHS.

Curran, Barbara A. "Dooley Cohort: Process and Results." 1995. MHF.

———. "Dooley Cohort Working List." 1995. MHF.

Dooley, James H. Last Will and Testament, 2 June 1919. Codicils 22 March 1920, 21 March 1921, and 15 November 1922. Probated Circuit Court, City of Richmond, Division 1, Virginia, 13 February 1923. Will Book 20, 34.

———. Papers. Branch and Company Records, 1837–1976. VHS.

Dooley, Sallie May. Last Will and Testament, 7 June 1923. Codicil 11 June 1924. Probated Circuit Court of Nelson County, Virginia, 17 September 1925. Will Book O, 281–99.

Easton, Evelyn Bridges. Letter to Dale Wheary, 22 July 1979. MHF.

Elder, Fitzhugh, Jr. Letter to Dale Wheary, 25 June 1998. MHF.

Ferris, Anne. "The Dooleys' Household Staff, 1880–1925." December 2000. MHF.

Hester, Roseann Tatum. Letter to Dale Wheary, 1993. MHF.

"Hostesses' Day Book, 1926–1961." MHA.

Logan, Kate V. to Sallie May Dooley, undated letter. MHA.

Lunenburg County, Virginia, Tax Lists 1836–1850. Library of Virginia. Microfilm reel no. 240.

McClenahan, Mary Tyler. Comments at Maymont African-American History Roundtable. 4 November 1994. MHF.

Phillips, Charles. "Maymont House, Richmond: Exploratory Investigation of Basement." 3 vols. Winston-Salem: Phillips and Oppermann, September 1997. MHL.

"Southern Negro Women and Race Cooperation." Southeastern Federation of Colored Women's Clubs, 1921. Maggie Lena Walker Papers, Box 4, Folder 5. Maggie L. Walker National Historic Site Archives.

Steltzner, Mildred White, and Lucille White Cutting, eds. *1850 Census of Lunenburg County, Virginia.* [1967].

Weis, Tracey M. "Negotiating Freedom: Domestic Service and the Landscape of Labor and Household Relations in Richmond, VA, 1850–1880." Ph.D. diss., Rutgers, State University of New Jersey, 1994.

Welsh, Frank S. "Microscopical paint and color analysis." Welsh Color and Conservation, Inc., 15 July 1997 and 10 October 2000. MHF.

Wheary, Dale. "Swannanoa: Summer Home of James and Sallie Dooley." Unpublished manuscript. April 2000. MHF.

Winn, Elizabeth Jarvis. "Memories of East Franklin Street." 1965. VHS.

"Women, Labor, and Working Conditions." In "Know Your City Study, 1911." File 21, YWCA Records. Special Collections, James Branch Cabell Library, Virginia Commonwealth University.

Woodson, Frances Ann. Oath of allegiance, witnessed by James H. Dooley, 19 October 1865. VHS.

Worthington, William E., Jr. "Report on Inspection of Maymont Household Systems." 18 September 1995. MHF.

Articles, Books, and Government Documents

"All One Family." *Richmond Planet,* 28 January 1899, 4.

Alsop, Benjamin Pollard, Jr. "Richmond Recollections." *Richmond Quarterly* 9 (Summer 1986): 25–45.

"American Millionaires. The Tribune's List of all Persons in the United States Reputed to be Worth a Million or More." *New York Tribune Monthly* 4 (June 1892).

"The American Negro." *Richmond Times,* 30 March 1900, 4.

Amott, Teresa, and Julie Matthaei. *Race, Gender, and Work: A Multi-Cultural Economic History of Women in the United States.* Boston: South End Press, 1991.

Anderson, C. Arnold, and Mary Jean Bowman. "The Vanishing Servant and the Contemporary Status System of the American South." *American Journal of Sociology* 59 (November 1953): 215–30.

Annual Report of the Superintendent of Public Instruction of the Commonwealth of Virginia. Vol. 6. October 1923.

Aslet, Clive. *The American Country House.* New Haven: Yale University Press, 1990.

"'Aunt Mary' Dead: She Was Respected and Esteemed Beyond Her Race." *Richmond Evening Leader,* 23 January 1899, 7.

Ayers, Edward L. *The Promise of the New South: Life After Reconstruction.* New York: Oxford University Press, 1984.

Baldwin, James. *The Fire Next Time.* New York: Dial, 1963.

Bauers, Sandy, and Stacey Burling. "Nanny works off the books." *Tacoma Morning News Tribune,* 21 February 1993, F-2, F-6.

Bayliss, Mary Lynn. "The Dooleys: A View from Their Library." *Richmond Quarterly* 8 (Summer 1986): 1–8.

Becker, Robert. *Nancy Lancaster: Her Life, Her World, Her Art.* New York: Alfred A. Knopf, 1996.

Beeman, Richard R. *The Evolution of the Southern Backcountry: A Case Study of Lunenburg County, Virginia, 1746–1832.* Philadelphia: University of Pennsylvania Press, 1984.

Bell, Landon. *The Old Free State, or Contribution to the History of Lunenburg County and Southside Virginia.* Richmond: William Byrd Press, 1927.

Beney, M. Ada. *Wages, Hours, and Employment in the United States, 1914–36.* New York: National Industrial Conference Board, 1936.

Blair, Lewis H. *The Prosperity of the South Dependent upon the Elevation of the Negro.* Richmond: Everett Waddey, 1889.

"Book Notes." *Richmond News Leader,* 3 November 1906, 7.

Bowen, Barbara Trigg. "My Friend, Nannie Langhorne—Lady Astor."

Richmond Quarterly 2 (Winter 1988), 10–17.

Brown, Elsa Barkley, and Gregg D. Kimball. "Mapping the Terrain of Black Richmond." *Journal of Urban History* 21 (March 1995): 296–346.

Campbell, Helen. *Household Economics.* New York: C. Putnam's Sons, 1897.

———. *Women Wage-Earners: Their Past, Their Present, and Their Future.* 1893. Reprint, New York: Arno Press, 1972.

"Candidates for Office." *Richmond Daily Dispatch,* 16 October 1877, 2.

Caravati, Charles M. *Major Dooley.* Richmond: [published for the Maymont Foundation], 1978.

Cashman, Sean Dennis. *America in the Gilded Age: From the Death of Lincoln to the Rise of Theodore Roosevelt.* 2d ed. New York: New York University Press, 1988.

Catalogue of the Officers and Students of Hartshorn Memorial College, 1886–87. Richmond: Hartshorne Memorial College, 1887.

Chase, Fannie Dickerson. *Good Form and Social Ethics.* Washington, D.C.: Review and Herald Publishing Association, 1913.

Chataigne's City Directory of Richmond. Richmond: J. H. Chataigne, 1885–86.

Chataigne's City Directory of Richmond. Richmond: J. H. Chataigne, 1893.

Chesnutt, Charles W. *The Marrow of Tradition.* 1901. Reprint, Ann Arbor: The University of Michigan Press, 1973.

Bibliography

_____

Chesson, Michael B. *Richmond after the War, 1865–1890.* Richmond: Virginia State Library, 1981.

Christian, W. Asbury. *Richmond: Her Past and Present.* Richmond: L. H. Jenkins, 1912.

Clark-Lewis, Elizabeth. *Living In, Living Out: African American Domestics in Washington, D.C., 1910–1940.* Washington, D.C., and London: Smithsonian Institution Press, 1994.

Clinton, Catherine. *Tara Revisited: Women, War, and the Plantation Legend.* New York: Abbeville Press, 1995.

Constitution of Virginia. Richmond: n.p., 1876.

Coontz, Stephanie. *The Social Origins of Private Life: A History of American Families 1600–1900.* New York: Verso, 1988.

Copeland, Elizabeth, and Anne Wayland. "Lovely Garden of 'Maymont' Was Planned by the Wife of Major Dooley." *Richmond Times-Dispatch,* 9 July 1933, V-3.

"The Correct Aprons for Maids." *Ladies Home Journal* (March 1910): 47.

Corson, Juliet. *Miss Corson's Practical American Cookery.* New York: Dodd, Mead, and Co., 1885.

Cowan, Ruth Schwartz. *More Work for Mother: The Ironies of Household Technology from the Open Hearth to the Microwave.* New York: Basic Books, 1983.

Cronly, Martha Valentine. "I Remember It Well: Richmond in the Early 1900s." *Richmond Quarterly* 5 (Summer 1982): 42–44.

Cushing, Ethel Frey. *Culture and Good Manners.* Memphis, Tenn.: Students Educational Publishing Co., 1926.

Cutchins, John A. *Memories of Old Richmond, 1881–1944.* Verona, Va.: McClure Press, 1974.

Dabney, Virginius. *Richmond: The Story of a City.* Garden City, N.Y.: Doubleday and Co., 1976.

———. *Virginia: The New Dominion.* New York: Doubleday and Co., 1971.

Dailey, Jane. *Before Jim Crow: The Politics of Race in Postemancipation Virginia.* Chapel Hill and London: The University of North Carolina Press, 2000.

Degler, Carl N. *At Odds: Women and the Family in America from the Revolution to the Present.* New York: Oxford University Press, 1980.

Denslow, Van Buren. "The Ideal and Practical Organization of a Home." *Cosmopolitan* 27 (May 1899): 52.

Dolley, Charles S., M.D. *The Technology of Bacteria Investigation.* Boston: S. E. Cassino and Co., 1885.

Dooley, James. "To Messrs. A. M. Keiley, Joseph R. Anderson, W. W. Crump, and Others." *Richmond Daily Dispatch,* 19 October 1877, 1.

Dooley, John. *John Dooley, Confederate Soldier: His War Journal.* Edited by Joseph T. Durkin. Washington, D.C.: Georgetown University Press, 1945.

Dooley, Mrs. James H. *Dem Good Ole Times.* New York: Doubleday, Page and Co., 1906.

"Dooley's Diagnosis." *Richmond Daily Dispatch,* 30 July 1893, 2.

Douglas, Paul H. *Real Wages in the United States, 1890–1926.* Boston: Houghton Mifflin Co., 1930.

Du Bois, W. E. Burghardt. *Black Reconstruction in America: An Essay Toward a History of the Part Which Black Folk Played in the Attempt to Reconstruct Democracy in America, 1860–1880.* 1935. Reprint, New York: Russell and Russell, 1963.

———. *Darkwater: Voices from Within the Veil.* 1920. Reprint, New York: Schocken Books, 1969.

———. *The Negro Church: A Social Study.* Atlanta: Atlanta University Press, 1903.

———. "The Negroes of Farmville, Virginia: A Social Study." *Bulletin of the Department of Labor* 3, January 1898.

———. *Pamphlets and Leaflets by W. E. B. Du Bois.* Edited by Herbert Aptheker. White Plains, N.Y.: Kraus-Thomson Organization, 1986.

———. *The Philadelphia Negro: A Social Study.* 1899. Reprint, New York: Schocken Books, 1967.

———. *The Souls of Black Folk.* 1903. Reprint, Chicago: A. C. McClurg, 1909.

Dudden, Faye. *Serving Women: Household Service in Nineteenth-Century America.* Middletown, Conn.: Wesleyan University Press, 1983.

Duke, Maurice, and Daniel P. Jordan, eds. *A Richmond Reader, 1733–1983.* Chapel Hill: University of North Carolina Press, 1983.

Dunbar, Paul Laurence. "We Wear the Mask." *Lyrics of Lowly Life.* New York: Dodd, Mead, and Co., 1898.

Earnest, Joseph B. *The Religious Development of the Negro in Virginia.* Charlottesville: Michie Co., 1914.

Ellison, Ralph. *Invisible Man.* New York: Random House, 1952.

Epps, Clara Becker. "2501 Grove Avenue: 1889–1914." *Richmond Quarterly* 12 (Spring 1990): 36–37.

"Farm Hands to Get Ginter's Money." *Richmond News Leader,* 9 December 1903, 1.

"Finest Residences." *Richmond State,* 31 January 1886, 4.

Fleming, Walter L. "The Servant Problem in a Black Belt Village." *The Sewanee Review* 13 (January 1905): 1–17.

Fothergill, Augusta B. *Peter Jones and Richard Jones Genealogies.* Richmond: Old Dominion Press, 1924.

Frederickson, George M. *The Black Image in the White Mind: The Debate on Afro-American Character and Destiny, 1817–1914.* New York: Harper Torchbooks, 1971.

Gavins, Raymond. *The Perils and Prospects of Southern Black Leadership: Gordon Blain Hancock, 1884–1970.* Durham, N.C.: Duke University Press, 1977.

Gee, Wilson, and John J. Corson. *A Statistical Study of Virginia.* Charlottesville: Charlottesville Institute for Research in Social Sciences, University of Virginia, 1927.

Gibson, Langhorne, Jr. *The Gibson Girl: Portrait of a Southern Belle.* Richmond: Commodore Press, 1997.

———. *My Precious Husband: The Story of Elise & Fred Scott.* [S. L.]: Cadmus Fine Books, 1994.

Ginger, Ray. *Age of Excess: The United States from 1877 to 1914.* New York: Macmillan, 1965.

Gossett, Thomas F. *Race: The History of an Idea in America.* Dallas: Southern Methodist University Press, 1963.

Green, Harvey. *The Light of the Home: An Intimate View of the Lives of Women in Victorian America.* New York: Pantheon Books, 1983.

Greenwald, John. "The Price of Obeying the Law." *Time,* 1 February 1993, 34–35.

Gunning, Sandra. *Race, Rape, and Lynching: The Red Record of American Literature, 1890–1912.* New York: Oxford University Press, 1996.

"Harmful Rush of Negro Workers to the North." *Richmond Planet,* 23 June 1917, 1.

Hart, Lavinia. "What a Mother Can Do for Her Daughter." *Cosmopolitan* 24 (December 1902): 158–62.

Haynes, Elizabeth Ross. "Negroes in Domestic Service." *Journal of Negro History* 8 (October 1923): 384–442.

Henderson, Mrs. Mary F. *Practical Cooking and Dinner Giving.* New York: Harper and Brothers, 1887.

"History and Tradition Favored Richmond Bank. Major Dooley's Letter to Comptroller Williams Dwelt on Strong Bond Between South, and One-Time Capital of the Confederacy." *Richmond Times-Dispatch*, 3 April 1914, 5.

Holt, Emily. *Everyman's Encyclopaedia of Etiquette.* 1901. Reprint, New York: Doubleday, Page, and Co., 1920.

Home and Health. Nashville: Southern Publishing Association, 1907.

Hunter, Tera W. *To 'Joy My Freedom: Southern Black Women's Lives and Labors after the Civil War.* Cambridge, Mass.: Harvard University Press, 1998.

"Jane Minor." *Richmond Times-Dispatch*, 23 February 1999, D-1.

Jones, Jacqueline. *Labor of Love, Labor of Sorrow: Black Women, Work, and the Family from Slavery to the Present.* New York: Basic Books, 1985.

Journal of House of Delegates of the State of Virginia, for the Session of 1871–72. Richmond: Clemitt and Jones, 1872.

Kaplan, Amy. "Nation, Region, and Empire." In *Columbia History of the American Novel,* edited by Emory Elliott, 240–66. New York: Columbia University Press, 1991.

Katzman, David. *Seven Days a Week: Women and Domestic Service in Industrializing America.* Urbana: University of Illinois Press, 1981.

"Keep the Races Apart." *Richmond Times*, 12 January 1900, 4.

King, Mrs. J. A. *An Afternoon with Hartshorn Memorial College.* Boston: Woman's American Baptist Home Mission Society, ca. 1891.

Knight, Charles Louis. *Negro Housing in Certain Virginia Cities.* Richmond: William Byrd Press, 1927.

"Ku Klux Klan Secret Organization Parade the Streets of Richmond." *Richmond Planet*, 11 December 1920, 1.

Lancaster, Nancy. "Richmond, 1903–1913." *Richmond Quarterly* 4 (Summer 1981): 34–39.

Langhorne, Orra. "Domestic Service in the South." *Journal of Social Science* 39 (November 1901): 169–75.

———. *Southern Sketches from Virginia, 1881–1901.* Edited by Charles E. Wynes. Charlottesville: University Press of Virginia, 1964.

Lebsock, Suzanne. *The Free Women of Petersburg: Status and Culture in a Southern Town, 1784–1760.* New York: W. W. Norton, 1984.

"Legacies to Servants." *New York Law Journal*, 10 February 1904, 1624.

Lemons, J. Stanley. "Black Stereotypes as Reflected in Popular Culture, 1880–1920." *American Quarterly* 29 (Spring 1977): 102–16.

Leonard, Margaret. "How He Knocked Out Sullivan is Retold by Richmond Negro." *Richmond Times-Dispatch*, 28 July 1936, 4.

Levenstein, Harvey A. *Revolution at the Table: The Transformation of the American Diet.* New York: Oxford University Press, 1988.

Litwack, Leon. *Trouble in Mind: Black Southerners in the Age of Jim Crow.* New York: Alfred A. Knopf, 1998.

Locke, Alain. *The Negro in Art: A Pictorial Record of the Negro Artist and of the Negro Theme in Art.* Washington, D.C.: Associates in Negro Folk Education, 1940.

"Lunenburg County, Virginia, 1800 Tax List." *Virginia Genealogist* 38 (July–September 1994): 221–26.

Lynes, Russell. *The Domesticated Americans.* New York: Harper and Row, 1963.

Mackay, Charles. *Life and Liberty in America; or, Sketches of a Tour in the United States and Canada in 1857–1858.* Vol. 1. 1859. Reprint, New York: Johnson Reprint Co., 1971.

Maddex, Jack P., Jr. *Virginia Conservatives, 1867–1879.* Chapel Hill: University of North Carolina Press, 1970.

"Major Dooley Pays Fine Tribute to Richmond." *Richmond Times,* 27 June 1902, 3.

"Major J. H. Dooley Dies in 83rd Year." *Richmond Times-Dispatch,* 17 November 1922, 1.

Mann, Etta Donnan. *Four Years in the Governor's Mansion of Virginia, 1910–1914.* Richmond: Dietz Press, 1937.

Matthews, Glenna. *"Just a Housewife": The Rise and Fall of Domesticity in America.* New York: Oxford University Press, 1987.

McCabe, Gordon. *Joseph Bryan: A Brief Memoir.* Richmond: Virginia Historical Society, 1909.

McClure, Abbot, and Harold Donaldson Eberlein. *House Furnishing and Decoration.* New York: McBride, Nast and Co., 1914.

McLeod, Norman C., Jr. "Not Forgetting the Land We Left: The Irish in Antebellum Richmond." *Virginia Cavalcade* 47 (Winter 1998): 36–47.

"Meeting of Irish Citizens." *Richmond Daily Dispatch,* 13 June 1868, 2.

Meier, August, and Elliott Rudwick. "Negro Boycotts of Segregated Streetcars in Virginia, 1904–1907." *Virginia Magazine of History and Biography* 81 (October 1973): 479–87.

Miller, Elizabeth Smith. *In the Kitchen.* New York: Henry Holt, 1883.

Miller, Zane L. "Urban Blacks in the South, 1865–1920: The Richmond, Savannah, New Orleans, Louisville and Birmingham Experience." In *The New Urban History,* edited by Leo F. Schnore, 184–204. Princeton: Princeton University Press, 1975.

Moody, Helen Watterson. *The Unquiet Sex.* New York: Charles Scribner's Sons, 1898.

"Mrs. Dooley's Reception: One of the Most Brilliant Events of the Season." *Richmond Times-Dispatch,* 10 February 1898, 2.

"The Negro Exodus to the North is a Very Serious Menace to the Southland." *Richmond Planet,* 28 April 1917, 1.

The Negro in Richmond, Virginia. Richmond: Richmond Council of Social Agencies, 1929.

The Negro in Virginia. 1940. Reprint, Winston-Salem, N.C.: John F. Blair, 1994.

O'Leary, Elizabeth L. *At Beck and Call: The Representation of Domestic Servants in Nineteenth-Century American Painting.* Washington D.C.: Smithsonian Institution Press, 1996.

Page, Thomas Nelson. "The Lynching of Negroes—Its Cause and Its Prevention." *North American Review* 566 (January 1904): 33–48.

———. *The Negro: The Southerner's Problem.* New York: Charles Scribner's Sons, 1904.

Palmer, Phyllis. *Domesticity and Dirt: Housewives and Domestic Servants in the United States, 1920–1945*. Philadelphia: Temple University Press, 1989.

"Parade of History: Tales Recapture Franklin Street's Sociable Past." *Richmond News Leader*, 17 August 1977, 35.

Perdue, Charles L., Thomas E. Barden, and Robert K. Phillips, eds. *Weevils in the Wheat: Interviews with Virginia Ex-Slaves*. Charlottesville: University Press of Virginia, 1976.

Pettengill, Lillian. *Toilers of the Home: The Record of a College Woman's Experience as Domestic Servant*. New York: Doubleday, Page and Co., 1903.

Population Schedules of the Twelfth Census of the United States, 1850. New York, New York County, New York City, Ward 14. Microfilm roll 551. Washington D.C.: National Archives, 1963.

"Proposed Remedy for the Negro Exodus." *Richmond Planet*, 5 May 1917, 1.

Rachleff, Peter J. *Black Labor in the South: Richmond, Virginia, 1865–1890*. Philadelphia: Temple University Press, 1984.

Report of the Labor Commissioner, Bureau of Labor and Industrial Statistics of the State of Virginia. Richmond: Davis Bottom, Superintendent of Public Printing, 1923.

"Review and Magazine Notes." *Times-Dispatch*, 28 October, 1906, E-7.

Richardson, Archie G. *The Development of Negro Education in Virginia, 1831–1970*. Richmond: Phi Delta Kappa, 1976.

Richmond City Directory. Richmond: Hill Directory, 1913.

Richmond Elite Directory (Blue Book). Richmond: J. L. Hill Printing Co., 1893.

Rollins, Judith. *Between Women: Domestics and Their Employers*. Philadelphia: Temple University Press, 1985.

Rubinow, I. M., and Daniel Durant. "The Depth and Breadth of the Servant Problem." *McClure's Magazine* 34 (March 1910): 576–85.

Ryan, John A. *A Living Wage*. New York: Macmillan Co., 1920.

Salmon, Lucy Maynard. *Domestic Service*. 1897. Reprint: New York: Arno Press, 1972.

Scott, Mary Wingfield. *Old Richmond Neighborhoods*. Richmond: Whittet and Shepperson, 1950.

———. "712 . . . Hail and Farewell." Richmond: [n.p.], 1950.

"Servants to be Paid." *Times-Dispatch*, 10 December 1903, 9.

Shaw, Stephanie J. *What a Woman Ought to Be and to Do: Black Professional Women Workers During the Jim Crow Era*. Chicago: University of Chicago Press, 1996.

Sherman, Richard B. "'The Last Stand': The Fight for Racial Integrity in Virginia in the 1920s." *Journal of Southern History* 54 (February 1988): 69–92.

"Social Security Domestic Employment Reform Act of 1994." Report 103–252. *Senate Reports, Nos. 251–282*, United States Congressional Serial Set, Serial Number 14222. Washington, D.C.: U.S. Government Printing Office, 1996.

Spofford, Harriet Prescott. *The Servant Girl Question*. 1881. Reprint, New York: Arno Press, 1977.

Stevenson, Brenda E. *Life in Black and White: Family and Community in the Slave South*. New York: Oxford University Press, 1996.

Story, Josephine. "How I Kept House Without a Servant." *Richmond Times-Dispatch*, 8 March 1914, feature section, 5.

Strasser, Susan. *Never Done: A History of American Housework*. New York: Pantheon Books, 1982.

Sutherland, Daniel E. *Americans and Their Servants: Domestic Service in the United States from 1800 to 1920*. Baton Rouge: Louisiana State University Press, 1981.

————. "Modernizing Domestic Service." In *American Home Life, 1880–1930: A Social History of Spaces and Services*, edited by Jessica Foy and Thomas J. Schlereth, 242–65. Knoxville: University of Tennessee Press, 1992.

Sykes, Christopher. *Nancy: The Life of Lady Astor*. Chicago: Academy Chicago, 1984.

Terrell, Mary Church. "Lynching from a Negro's Point of View." *North American Review* 571 (June 1904): 853–68.

Thirty-Ninth Annual Report of the Superintendent of the Public Schools of the City of Richmond, Virginia for the Scholastic Year Ending July 31, 1908. Richmond: Clyde W. Saunders, City Printer, 1909.

Thirty-Seventh Annual Catalogue of Hampton Institute. Hampton, Va.: The Institute Press, 1905.

Trachtenberg, Alan. *The Incorporation of America: Culture and Society in the Gilded Age*. New York: Hill and Wang, 1982.

Turner, E. S. *What the Butler Saw: Two Hundred and Fifty Years of the Servant Problem*. New York: St. Martin's Press, 1963.

Twelfth Census of the United States, 1900. Virginia, Henrico County, Tuckahoe District. Microcopy no. T623, reel no. 1712.

Tyler-McGraw, Marie. *At the Falls: Richmond, Virginia, and Its People*. Chapel Hill: University of North Carolina Press, 1994.

Veblen, Thorstein. *The Theory of the Leisure Class*. 1899. Reprint, New York: Penguin Books, 1979.

Villard, Oswald Garrison. "The Negro and the Domestic Problem." *Alexander's Magazine* 1 (15 November 1905): 5–11.

Virginia Slave Schedules [of the Eighth Census of the United States], 1860. National Archives microcopy 653, roll 1391, Library of Virginia microfilm reel 226e, 041.

"Wanted Negro Domestics: Members of Housewive's League Are Behind Movement." *People's Pilot* 1 (May 1919): 27, 39.

Washington, Booker T. *Up from Slavery: An Autobiography*. Garden City, N.Y.: Doubleday, Page and Co., 1900.

Wheary, Dale. "Maymont: Gilded Age Estate." *Maymont Notes* 1 (Fall 2001): 9–14.

Williams, Murat. "'Aunt' Charlotte, in River Road Cottage, Tells of Cooking for Two U.S. Presidents." *Richmond News Leader*, 17 April 1936, 10.

Woloch, Nancy. *Women and the American Experience*. New York: Alfred A. Knopf, 1984.

Woodson, Carter G. *A Century of Negro Migration*. Washington, D.C.: Association for the Study of Negro Life and History, 1918.

————. "The Negro Washerwoman, A Vanishing Figure." *Journal of Negro History* 15 (July 1930): 269–77.

Woodward, C. Vann. *The Strange Career of Jim Crow*. 3d ed. New York: Oxford University Press, 1974.

Wright, Mrs. Julia McNair. *The Complete Home: An Encyclopaedia of Domestic Life and Affairs*. Richmond: B. F. Johnson and Co., 1883.

Wynes, Charles E. *Race Relations in Virginia, 1870–1902*. Charlottesville: University of Virginia Press, 1961.

ployers, 53-54, 122-23; contracting for, 81; day work, 106-7, 118; deferential demeanor of, 85-87; female workers, 80-81; hours and days of work, 105-6, 107-8; intercessions for, by employers, 44-45; male workers, 24, *64*; migration north, 99-101; mobility of workers following Civil War, 151 n. 15; paternalism and deference in, 42-43; perceived assertiveness of workers, 43; prevalence of black workers, 40, 42; "Servant Problem," 42, 55; terminology for, 35-38, 89-90; training of, 94-99; twentieth-century changes, 118-19. *See also* domestic labor (slave)

domestic labor (U.S.): associated with domestic labor of African Americans, 40, 82; attempts to reform, 96; day work, 106, 118; fluidity of work duties, 110; governmental regulation and taxation of wages, 118, 164 n. 111; immigrant work force, 37; interstaff relationships, 109-10; "invisibility" of workers, 17-18, 119; job training, 94-99; labor unions for, 117; living in, 102-5; living out, 105-6; male workers, 24; mobility of workers, 87, 102, 151 n. 15; non-monetary wages, 112-13, 115-17; personal freedom of workers, 102-3, 104-5; prevalence of, 22; relationships between employer and employee, 83; "Servant Problem," 38-40; stigma of, 37, 82; terminology for workers, 35-38, 89, 155 nn. 86, 88; in upper-class residences, 23-24; wages, 111; work and living spaces for workers, 17, 104; worker rejection of term "servant," 89-90; workers as status symbols, 24-26, 34; workers considered "one of the family," 121-24. *See also* uniforms

domestic labor (Virginia): benefits, 112-13, 115-17; care of workers' children, 106; employment agencies, 99-100, 161 n. 58; employment networks, 99; female workers, 80-82, 153 n. 42; hours and days of work, 105-6, 107-8; immigrant employees, 41-42; labor unions, 117-18; male workers, 24, 80, 153 n. 45; migration north, 99-101; personal freedom of workers, 104-5; prevalence of African Americans, 40; relationships between employers and em-

ployees, 53-54, 83-84, *67*; in Richmond, 23, 40-41, 53, 80, 99, 111; terminology, 35-38, 89-90; training of workers, 94-99; uniforms, 34-35, 62, 91-92; wages, 111-12; white employees, 41, 156 n. 104

domestic science training, *69*, 96-98

Donnan, Cleiland, 54, 86

Dooley, Alice, 132

Dooley, James Henry, *58*; academic achievements, 12; as "capitalist," 12, 150 n. 4; charitable giving, 5, 50-51, 124; childhood of, 11, 19-20; and the Civil War, 12, 33, 58, 150 n. 3; Irish ancestry, 11, 42, 48; law training and career, 12, 15; marketing for groceries, 76, 112-13; marriage to Sallie May, 14; —, and residence at 1 W. Grace Street, 15; —, and residence at 212 W. Franklin Street, 15-16, 151 n. 17; millionaire status, 16, 58, 151 n. 18; political activities, 47-50; temperament, described by employee, 51, 52; Westmoreland Club, founding member of, 64; witnesses oaths of allegiance, 15. *See also* domestic labor (Dooley employees); Dooley Papers; Maymont estate; Maymont House (Dooley residence); Swannanoa

Dooley, John, Jr., 12, 38

Dooley, John, Sr., 11-12, 14-15, 36

Dooley, Sarah (Mrs. John Dooley, Sr.), 11

Dooley, Sarah O. "Sallie" May: 1-4, 6, *58*; author of *Dem Good Ole Times*, 6, 14, 54-56, 58, 123; charitable giving, 5, 50, 124; childhood of, 12-14, 19-20; destruction of personal papers, 6, 57; entertaining at Maymont, 25, 29, 153 n. 47, 154 n. 57; fondness for swans, 27, 109, 162 n. 88; gardening activities, 27, 51-52, 140; marriage to James Henry Dooley, 14; —, and residence at 1 W. Grace Street, 15; —, and residence at 212 W. Franklin Street, 15-16, 151 n. 17; perceptions of antebellum plantation system, 13-14, 54; receiving visitors "at home," 25, 153 n. 47; temperament of, described by employee, 52; wardrobe of, 32-33, 65. *See also* domestic labor (Dooley employees); Maymont estate; Maymont House (Dooley residence); Swannanoa